What Really Happened?
─World Mysteries Solved─

ほんと？ うそ？ 世界の びっくり ミステリー

FRANK BAILEY
MIYO NOTOMI
HARUHIKO TAMIYA
TAKAKO TAKAMOTO

KAIBUNSHA LTD
TOKYO

音声ダウンロード（無料）は

http://www.kaibunsha.co.jp/download/16729 （リリースは 2016 年 4 月）

音声は上記 URL から無料でダウンロードできます。自習用としてご活用ください。

- URL は検索ボックスではなくアドレスバー（URL 表示枠）に入力してください。
- PC からのダウンロードをお勧めします。スマートフォンなどでおこないますと、3G 回線環境ではダウンロードできない場合があります。

まえがき

　みなさんは世界のあちこちに伝わる謎について聞いたことがあるでしょう。そして、それらのお話は本当なのか、不思議に思ったことがあるでしょう。たとえば……

「ナスカの地上絵は本当に宇宙人が手伝ったの？」
「ネス湖のネッシーって本当にいるの？」
「ツタンカーメンのミイラの呪いは本当なの？」

　実は、これらの謎はかなりの程度まで解き明かされています。この本で世界各地に伝わるさまざまな謎の答えを見つけましょう！

　どのエピソードも、日本での英語教育歴が長いアメリカ人大学教員フランク・ベイリーの書き下ろしで、読みやすい、やさしい英語で書かれています。各 Unit の**読解のポイント**と巻末の「**文法解説**」を参考にしながら読み進めてください。そのあとで Composition の問題を解きましょう。読解のポイントで学んだ知識を定着させることができます。また、Listening Comprehension や Dictation の問題は、リスニングの力をつけるだけではなく、基本的な単語のつづりを覚えるためのものです。発音を確かめながら、単語を覚えるようにしましょう。

　本書を使ってみなさんが楽しく英語を勉強してくれることを願っています。最後になりましたが、本書の作成にあたっては開文社出版社長の安居洋一氏、イラストを描いてくれた鈴木文生氏にたいへんお世話になりました。この場を借りてお礼申し上げます。

平成 27 年 10 月

著者一同

i

1– Nazca   2– Loch Ness   3– Bermuda Triangle
4– Himalayas   5– Mary Celeste   6– Egypt
7– Dyatlov Pass

目　次

まえがき ・・・・・・・・・・・・・・・・・・・・・・・・・・・・・・・・・・・・・・ i

基本的な文法事項 ・・・・・・・・・・・・・・・・・・・・・・・・・・・・・ 1

Unit 1　ナスカの地上絵【ミステリー編】(be 動詞) ・・・・・・・・・ 5

Unit 2　ナスカの地上絵【解決編】(be 動詞と一般動詞) ・・・・・ 9

Unit 3　ネス湖とネッシー【ミステリー編】(have, had) ・・・・・ 13

Unit 4　ネス湖とネッシー【解決編】(~ing) ・・・・・・・・・・ 17

Unit 5　魔のバミューダ海域【ミステリー編】(and / but / or) ・・・・・ 21

Unit 6　魔のバミューダ海域【解決編】(過去形と過去分詞形) ・・・ 25

Unit 7　ヒマラヤの雪男【ミステリー編】(to- 不定詞) ・・・・・・・・・ 29

Unit 8　ヒマラヤの雪男【解決編】(that) ・・・・・・・・・・・・・ 33

Unit 9　消えた乗組員の謎【ミステリー編】(節のつなげかた) ・・・・・ 37

Unit 10　消えた乗組員の謎【解決編】(助動詞の過去形) ・・・・・・・・ 41

Unit 11　ミイラの呪い【ミステリー編】(関係詞節) ・・・・・・・・ 45

Unit 12　ミイラの呪い【解決編】(前置詞句) ・・・・・・・・・・・・ 49

Unit 13　ディアトロフ峠殺人事件 Part 1 (コンマ) ・・・・・・・・ 53

Unit 14　ディアトロフ峠殺人事件 Part 2 (同じ形の名詞と動詞) ・・・・・ 57

巻末付録 1 　文法解説

文法解説Ⅰ　五文型 ・・・・・・・・・・・・・・・・・・・・・・・・・ 62

文法解説Ⅱ　時の表し方 ・・・・・・・・・・・・・・・・・・・・・・・ 63

　Ⅱ - 1　時の表し方 ①　現在形 ・・・・・・・・・・・・・・・・・・・・ 64

　Ⅱ - 2　時の表し方 ②　過去形 ・・・・・・・・・・・・・・・・・・・・ 65

　Ⅱ - 3　時の表し方 ③　未来の表現 ・・・・・・・・・・・・・・・・ 66

　Ⅱ - 4　時の表し方 ④　現在完了形 ・・・・・・・・・・・・・・・・ 67

　Ⅱ - 5　時の表し方 ⑤　過去完了形 ・・・・・・・・・・・・・・・・ 68

　Ⅱ - 6　時の表し方 ⑥　未来完了形 ・・・・・・・・・・・・・・・・ 69

　Ⅱ - 7　時の表し方 ⑦　進行形 ・・・・・・・・・・・・・・・・・・・・ 70

文法解説Ⅲ　名詞の働きをするもの ・・・・・・・・・・・・・・・・・・・・・・・・・・・・ 72
Ⅲ-**1**　名詞の働きをするもの ①　準動詞 ・・・・・・・・・・・・・・・・・・・・ 73
Ⅲ-**2**　名詞の働きをするもの ②　疑問詞＋ to- 不定詞 ・・・・・・・・・・ 74
Ⅲ-**3**　名詞の働きをするもの ③　節（that- 節など）・・・・・・・・・・・・・ 75
Ⅲ-**4**　名詞の働きをするもの ④　節（間接疑問）・・・・・・・・・・・・ 76
Ⅲ-**5**　名詞の働きをするもの ⑤　節（関係詞節）・・・・・・・・・・・・ 77

文法解説Ⅳ　名詞を修飾するもの ・・・・・・・・・・・・・・・・・・・・・・・・・・・・・・ 78
Ⅳ-**1**　名詞を修飾するもの ①　準動詞 ・・・・・・・・・・・・・・・・・・・・・ 79
Ⅳ-**2**　名詞を修飾するもの ②　関係代名詞 ・・・・・・・・・・・・・・・・ 80
Ⅳ-**3**　名詞を修飾するもの ③　前置詞＋関係代名詞 ・・・・・・・・・ 81
Ⅳ-**4**　名詞を修飾するもの ④　関係副詞 ・・・・・・・・・・・・・・・・・・・ 82

文法解説Ⅴ　名詞以外を修飾するもの ・・・・・・・・・・・・・・・・・・・・・・・・・ 83
Ⅴ-**1**　名詞以外を修飾するもの ①　副詞・副詞句 ・・・・・・・・・・・・ 83
Ⅴ-**2**　名詞以外を修飾するもの ②　分詞構文 ・・・・・・・・・・・・・・・ 84
Ⅴ-**3**　名詞以外を修飾するもの ③　副詞節 ・・・・・・・・・・・・・・・・・ 85

文法解説Ⅵ　助動詞 ・・・ 86
Ⅵ-**1**　助動詞 can, may, will ・・・・・・・・・・・・・・・・・・・・・・・・・・・・・・ 86
Ⅵ-**2**　助動詞 must, should, need ・・・・・・・・・・・・・・・・・・・・・・・・ 87

文法解説Ⅶ　受動態 ・・・ 88

文法解説Ⅷ　比較 ・・・ 89
Ⅷ-**1**　比較 ①　原級比較 ・・・・・・・・・・・・・・・・・・・・・・・・・・・・・・・ 89
Ⅷ-**2**　比較 ②　比較級、最上級 ・・・・・・・・・・・・・・・・・・・・・・・・・ 90

文法解説Ⅸ　仮定法 ・・・ 91
Ⅸ-**1**　仮定法 ①　仮定法過去・仮定法過去完了 ・・・・・・・・・・・ 91
Ⅸ-**2**　仮定法 ②　I wish ~ ・・・・・・・・・・・・・・・・・・・・・・・・・・・・・・・ 92

巻末付録 2　不規則動詞の活用一覧表 ・・・・・・・・・・・・・・・・・・・・・・・ 94

基本的な文法事項

　Unit 1 に入る前に、本書に出てくる基本的な文法事項を下にまとめておく。空欄に書き入れておいて、勉強を進めていくときに必要に応じて参照しよう。

1.　品詞

単語を〈語形〉、〈はたらき〉、〈意味〉などによって分類したもの。単語がもともと持っている性質。1つの単語が2つ以上の品詞を持つこともある。下の語群から選んで、表に書き入れよう。

品詞	説明	単語の例 （下から選んで書き入れよう）
	人や事物の名前や概念を表す。	desk,
	人や事物の性質を表す語。**名詞**の前に置かれたり、**補語**として機能する。	happy,
	人や事物の動作、状態を表す語。目的語を取るものと取らないものとがある。	write,
	語と語、句と句、節と節を結びつける。	because,
	名詞の前に置かれ、語、句、節を修飾する。	with,
	名詞以外のいろいろな語（句）を修飾する。	hardly,
	名詞の前に置き、**名詞**の意味をある程度限定する。	a, an, the のみ
	人に呼びかけたり、感動を表すために用いる。	hello,

語群：名詞・形容詞・動詞・副詞・前置詞・接続詞・冠詞・間投詞

単語の例：water, rich, operate, fortunately, and, round, at, on, during, bread, oh, early, music, lose

基本的な文法事項　1

※ 句とは、2つ以上の単語が集まって、ある品詞に相当する働きをもつもの。**名詞句、形容詞句、副詞句の3種類**がある。

　　例）名詞句　　a small dog

　　例）形容詞句　an apple in the basket

　　例）副詞句　　work very hard

　節とは、2つ以上の単語が集まって、文の一部を構成するとともに、それ自体の中に「**主語＋述語動詞**」をもっているもの。例）I think that he is honest.

※ 文法参考書などによく「**副詞節**」、「**形容詞句**」などの言葉が出てくるが、これはそれぞれ「**副詞の働きをする節**」、「**形容詞の働きをする句**」などの意味である。「**関係代名詞節**」は、関係代名詞を用いているのでそう呼ばれるが、名詞を修飾し、形容詞の働きをしていることから、「**形容詞節**」と呼ばれることもある。

2.　文の要素

単語を、文における役割によって分類したもの。よって、文がないところには《文の要素》は存在し得ない。下の語群から選んで、表に書き入れよう。

主語・述語・目的語・補語

文の要素	説明	対応する品詞
	普通文頭に来る。「〜は」、「〜が」の意味を持つ。	名詞
	「〜する」、「〜した」などの意味を持つ。	動詞
	他動詞の後に置かれ、「〜を」、「〜に」の意味を持つ。	名詞
	be動詞などの後ろに置かれ、文を成り立たせるために必要な語。主語や目的語の意味を補う。	名詞、形容詞

語群：主語・述語・目的語・補語

3. 品詞と文の要素の対応

簡単な英文の構造を見てみよう。

	I	**have**	**a**	**sister.**
文の要素	主語 (S)	述語 (V)		目的語 (O)
品詞	名詞	動詞		名詞

	I	**am**	**happy.**
文の要素	主語 (S)	述語 (V)	補語 (C)
品詞	名詞	動詞	形容詞

※ **SVOC** の **V(verb)** の日本語訳は「述語」ではなく「動詞」である。また、述語は常に動詞であることから、文法書では「述語」と記載されることはほとんどなく、「述語動詞」あるいは単に「動詞」と記載される。

参考までに、SVOC の英語を挙げておく。

S（主語）= subject

V（動詞）= verb

O（目的語）= object

C（補語）= complement

●気をつけよう●

(1) 副詞 (adverb) は常に修飾の役割しか持たず、文の要素になることはない。

(2) 形容詞 (adjective) は、文の要素になる場合とならない場合がある。

例）　I　　found　　a small dog.
　　主語　述語動詞　　　目的語
　　→ small は目的語 dog を修飾する役割。よって、**文の要素ではない**。

　　The dog　　is　　small.
　　主語　述語動詞　補語
　　→ small は補語。よって、**文の要素となる**。

基本的な文法事項　3

Unit 1

ナスカの地上絵【ミステリー編】

動詞の活用　次の表の空白に書き入れよう。

	原形	過去形	過去分詞形	意味
1	draw			描く
2	remove			取り除く
3	fly			
4	see			

読解のポイント　【be 動詞】

(かっこの数字は文法解説のページ。以下すべての UNIT について同様)

英文の中に be 動詞が出てきたら、次のどれかであることが多い。

① be 動詞＋名詞または形容詞
　　→　名詞・形容詞は補語。「〜である」　例）This **is** a cat.

② There is [was, are, were] ＋主語　→　「〜がある（あった）」
　　主語＋ be 動詞＋場所を表す言葉　→　「〜は…にある（あった）」
　　　　例）There **is** a pen on the desk. / Mother **is** in the kitchen.

③ be 動詞＋ ~ing
　　→　進行形「〜している最中だ、〜する予定だ」(pp. 70–71)
　　　　例）He **is studying** English. / He **is leaving** soon.

④ be 動詞＋過去分詞　→　受動態「〜された、されている」(p. 88)
　　　　例）This dress **was made** by my mother.

ナスカの地上絵【ミステリー編】　5

1 The Nazca Lines in Peru **are** one of the great mysteries of the world. Over 300 lines and pictures of animals **are** drawn on the ground in the Nazca Desert. There **are** 300 pictures of animals like monkeys, spiders, birds, and even a whale. They **are** 20–100 meters across. One line **is** nearly 15 kilometers long and perfectly straight! The lines **were** made by removing dark rocks from the light-colored ground. They **were** discovered by people flying over in airplanes in the 1920's.

2 Why **are** they a mystery? They **were** made by the Nazca Indians hundreds of years ago ... but the pictures can only **be** seen from the air! From the ground, they just look like crazy lines. How did the Nazca make pictures they could not see?

3 A book about the lines called *Chariots of the Gods?* became famous in 1968. It said that aliens helped the Nazca make the lines, and the lines and pictures **are** runways and parking areas for spaceships! They **are** big enough, and some Nazca art shows creatures coming from the sky. Many people believed the book.

runway = 滑走路

parking area = 駐機場
spaceship = 宇宙船
creatures coming from the sky = 空からやって来た生物

4 Scientists do not believe aliens helped, but could not explain the mystery. Two scientists built a simple hot-air balloon with local materials and showed that it **was** possible for the Nazca to fly. But there **are** no Nazca pictures of balloons, and not many people think they had them.

hot-air balloon = 熱気球
local = 地元の、地元で手に入る
material = 材料
it (is) possible for the Nazca to fly = ナスカ人が空を飛ぶのは可能だ（It は to fly を指す仮主語）

5 **Were** they runways for aliens? If not, how **were** they made?

Listening Comprehension

1〜3の音声を聴いて、本文の内容と合っている英文の番号を○で囲もう。
（1つとは限らない。）　　　1　　2　　3

【ヒント】　1 **very few ~** = ほんの少数の〜
　　　　　2 **prove** = 実証する

Composition

（　　）内のヒントを参考にして、{　　}の語または語句を並べかえて日本語の意味を表す英文を作ろう。

1. 10年前にはこの商店街にはたくさんのブティックがあった。（本文第1段落）

   There { boutiques / in / many / this shopping arcade / were } 10 years ago.

   ....

2. この鶴は1枚の紙を折って作りました。（本文第1段落）

   This { a piece of / by / folding / made / crane / was } paper.

   ....

3. ナスカの地上絵はここからでは見ることができません。（本文第2段落）

   The { be / cannot / from / here / seen / Nazca Lines }.

   ....

Dictation

6~8

次の英文は Listening Comprehension のスクリプトである。音声を聴いて、（　　）に書き入れよう。そして、本文の内容と合っているのは1～3のどれか確認しよう。（以下の UNIT についても同様）

1. Very few people (　　　　　) the Nazca Lines were (　　　　　) as runways for alien spaceships.

2. The two (　　　　　) proved that it was possible for Nazca people to (　　　　　) a hot-air balloon.

3. Nazca people (　　　　　) (　　　　　) of pictures of aliens and spaceships.

8　UNIT 1

Unit 2

ナスカの地上絵【解決編】

動詞の活用　次の表の空白に書き入れよう。

	原形	過去形	過去分詞形	意味
1	damage			損傷を与える
2	stick			はまり込ませる
3	use			
4	find			

読解のポイント　【be 動詞と一般動詞】

1 つの英文には動詞が 1 つ以上ある。動詞には be 動詞と一般動詞がある。英文を読むときには次の①〜④に注意しよう。

① 現在形 (p. 64)　例）He **is** a student. / I **study** English every day.
② 過去形 (p. 65)　例）He **was** a student. / I **studied** English yesterday.
③ 助動詞＋動詞の原形 (p. 66, pp. 86–87)　例）I **will be** a space pilot.
④ 完了形（have/has/had ＋過去分詞）(pp. 67–69)
　　例）Tom **has lost** his car key.

※ 次のものは動詞ではないので、注意すること。
　　to- 不定詞
　　~ing 形
　　過去分詞（過去形と同じ形であることが多い）
　　例）I like apple pies **made** by my mother.
　　　（made は apple pies を修飾）

ナスカの地上絵【解決編】　9

1 First, the lines **are** not very good runways. The ground in the desert **is** too soft for anything to land there. Spaceships **would have gotten** stuck! The lines **are** easy to damage. Cars and trucks can easily **destroy** them.

2 Second, the pictures **look** like other Nazca art. They **drew** many similar pictures, especially in temples. They **are** probably pictures of their gods. Maybe the pictures **were** made for the gods to see.

3 Third, people **can make** a very big picture without being able to see it. By measuring the angles and sizes of a small picture, you **can make** big pictures easily, using wood poles and string to keep the lines straight. In 1982, a man named Joe Nickell **made** a copy of one of the Nazca pictures. He **used** only a small drawing, string and wooden sticks. In only two days he **made** a picture of a bird 150 meters across. A friend **flew** over in a plane and **took** pictures. The picture **was** perfect! He **showed** that the Nazca Indians **needed** only simple tools to make the picture. Later, small holes for wooden poles **were** found at Nazca!

4 The Nazca Lines **are** amazing, and we still **don't know** exactly why they **were** made. But no aliens or aircraft **were** needed. The Nazca **did** it with hard work and good planning. People in the past **did not have** airplanes or computers, but they **were** just as smart as we **are**.

tool = 道具

amazing = 驚くべき

exactly = 正確に

aircraft = 航空機（飛行機・飛行船・気球・ヘリコプターなどの総称）

in the past = 過去の

as smart as ~ = 〜と同じくらい頭が良い (p.89)

Listening Comprehension

1〜3の音声を聴いて、本文の内容と合っている英文の番号を○で囲もう。
（1つとは限らない。） 　　1　　2　　3

【ヒント】 3 ~ enough to- 不定詞 = 〜するほど十分に〜

ナスカの地上絵【解決編】 11

Composition

（　）内のヒントを参考にして、{　}の語または語句を並べかえて日本語の意味を表す英文を作ろう。

1. その鳥はまるで大きなコウモリのように見えた。（本文第2段落）
   { a / bat / big / bird / like / looked / the }.

2. 渡辺謙という名前の俳優を知っていますか。（本文第3段落）
   { an actor / do / Ken Watanabe / know / named / you }?

3. フレンチ・トーストをつくるには、卵1つと牛乳4分の1カップが必要です。（本文第3段落）
   You { and / a quarter cup / of milk / need / to / an egg } make French toast.

Dictation

音声を聴いて、（　）に書き入れよう。

1. Joe Nickell showed that it was (　　　) to draw giant pictures with (　　　) tools.

2. The Nazca Lines are drawn on the hard (　　　), so they are not easily (　　　).

3. Nazca people were not (　　　) enough to make big (　　　).

Unit 3

ネス湖とネッシー【ミステリー編】

動詞の活用　次の表の空白に書き入れよう。

	原形	過去形	過去分詞形	意味
1	swim			
2	raise			持ち上げる
3	sink			沈む、沈める
4	say			

読解のポイント　　【have, had】

have / has / had が出てきたら、次のどれかであることが多い。

① 後ろに名詞が来る　→　「持っている」などの意味の一般動詞
　　例）He **has** 10 pairs of shoes. / I **had** a good time.

② have [has, had] ＋ 過去分詞　→　完了形「〜した」(pp. 67–68)
　　例）He **has** already **finished** the homework.

③ have ＋物＋動詞の過去分詞／ have ＋人＋動詞の原形
　　→　使役構文「〜してもらう、〜される」
　　例）I **had** my room cleaned. / I **had** my son do the shopping.

④ have [has, had] ＋ to- 不定詞　→　〈義務〉を表す (p. 87)
　　例）I **have to do** my homework now.「〜しなければならない」

ネス湖とネッシー【ミステリー編】　13

1 In 1933, a man from London visited Loch Ness, a beautiful lake in Scotland. He was surprised to see something strange swimming in the lake. It looked like a plesiosaur, a dinosaur that **had** lived in the sea! It raised its head out of the water for a short time, then sank back into the lake. The dinosaurs all died 65,000,000 years ago. Did he really see a dinosaur?

2 After this many other people said they **had** seen the same animal. It was named the Loch Ness Monster, or "Nessie". The monster made the lake very famous. Many people still travel to the lake, hoping to see Nessie. Some people **have** taken pictures and even films that they say are the monster. These pictures and films are never very clear, and some were made as jokes. But people still sometimes say they **have** seen the monster.

3 Is Nessie a dinosaur? Did a group of plesiosaurs somehow keep living in Loch

---

loch = 湖（スコットランド・ゲール語）
see ＋人・物＋ ~ing = （人・物）が～しているのを見る
plesiosaur = プレシオサウルス、首長竜
dinosaur = 恐竜
a plesiosaur, a dinosaur ....
→ コンマは〈同格〉を表す。「すなわち」

65,000,000 = sixty-five million

make the lake very famous = その湖をとても有名にする (p. 62)
hoping to see Nessie = ネッシーを見たいと思いながら

film = 動画
they say = 彼らの言うところの【挿入句】
never [not] very ~ = あまり～ない
as ~ = ～として【前置詞】

somehow = なんとかして
keep ~ing = ～し続ける

Ness, eating fish and **having** babies for all those years? The lake is deep, and the water is very dark and hard to see through.

4 In 1985, a scientist used cameras and sonar to find the monster. He took a picture that looked like a fin! But there was only one picture and no one else **has** ever been able to take a clear picture of the monster. So what is the truth? Are there dinosaurs in a lake in Scotland?

for all those years = それまでの長い年月の間ずっと

hard to- 不定詞 = 〜するのがむずかしい
see through = 見通す
sonar = ソナー（音波の反射による水中障害物や海底状況探知装置）
fin = ひれ

no one else = 他のだれも（〜ない）

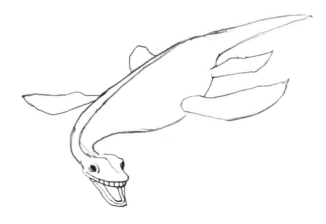

Listening Comprehension

1〜3の音声を聴いて、本文の内容と合っている英文の番号を○で囲もう。
（1つとは限らない。） 　　　1　　2　　3

【ヒント】 1 **Scotsman** = スコットランド人

Composition

（　　）内のヒントを参考にして、{　　　}の語または語句を並べかえて日本語の意味を表す英文を作ろう。

1. 姉も私も海外旅行をしたことがない。(neither ~ nor … = ～も…も―ない)
   (p. 13 読解のポイント)

   Neither { have / I / my / nor / sister / traveled } abroad.

   ....

2. その時までだれも彼の病気のことを聞いたことがなかった。
   (p. 13 読解のポイント)

   Until { of / his disease / had / heard / nobody / then }.

   ....

3. 今日のパーティは楽しかったですか。(p. 13 読解のポイント)

   { a good time / at / did / have / the party / you }?

   ....

Dictation

20~22

音声を聴いて、(　　)に書き入れよう。

1. A Scotsman visited Loch Ness and (　　　　　　　　) people that he had
   (　　　　　　) something like a dinosaur.

2. A scientist used sonar and took a clear picture of the (　　　　　　　) of the
   (　　　　　　).

3. The (　　　　　　) of Loch Ness isn't clear enough for us to see (　　　　　　)
   to the bottom.

16　UNIT 3

Unit 4

ネス湖とネッシー【解決編】

動詞の活用　次の表の空白に書き入れよう。

	原形	過去形	過去分詞形	意味
1	breathe			
2	put			(ある場所に) 持っていく、置く
3	get			手に入れる、移動する（させる）、〜の状態になる（する）
4	freeze			凍る、凍らせる

読解のポイント　【〜 ing】

~ing が出てきたら、次のどれであるかを考えよう。

① be 動詞＋ ~ing　→　進行形「〜している（いた）最中だ」(p. 70–71)
　　例）I **am studying** English.

② 前か後ろに名詞
　　→　~ing は名詞を修飾する現在分詞「〜しているところの」(p. 79)
　　例）Look at the **baby sleeping** in the bed.

③ **see, hear** ＋目的語＋ ~ing　→　~ing は目的補語（現在分詞）
　「〜が…しているのを見る（聞く）」など
　　例）I **heard a bird singing** in the tree.

④ 主語・目的語・補語になる　→　動名詞「〜する（した）こと」(p. 73)
　　例）I like **playing** the piano.

⑤ コンマを伴い、主節との間がコンマで区切られている
　　→　分詞構文「〜しているときに、〜したので、〜したら、〜しながら」
　　　　など (p. 84)
　　例）**Listening to the radio,** I studied for the exam.

ネス湖とネッシー【解決編】　17

1 There are no dinosaurs in Loch Ness. There are three big reasons why.

2 First, the lake is too small. There are not many fish or other animals in Loch Ness. A large animal like a dinosaur cannot live with such a small amount of food to eat.

3 Second, plesiosaurs were not fish. They breathed air, like a dolphin. So they had to put their heads out of the water a lot! People have lived near Loch Ness for hundreds of years, but nobody saw anything until Nessie was reported in 1933.

4 Third, scientists say the lake is only 30,000 years old, and for 20,000 years it was frozen! Plesiosaurs died 65,000,000 years ago. They were all dead a long time before Loch Ness was there.

5 So what are people **seeing**? Are they really **seeing** anything? Well, some of the stories are just not true. They are told for fun, or to get tourists to come to the lake.

6 Other people are not **lying**, but they didn't see a dinosaur! They saw things like **floating** logs, waves, and seals. The weather is often bad at Loch Ness, so it's hard to get a clear view. If people go to the lake **hoping** to see Nessie and see something **moving** in the water, they are likely to think they saw Nessie. Our mind can often trick us, especially if we want to be tricked.

lying < lie

log = 丸太
seal = あざらし

hope to- 不定詞 = 〜したいと願う

be likely to- 不定詞 = 〜しがちである

want to- 不定詞 = 〜したい

Listening Comprehension

1〜3の音声を聴いて、本文の内容と合っている英文の番号を○で囲もう。
（1つとは限らない。）　　　1　　2　　3

【ヒント】　1 **live on** ~ = 〜を常食にする
　　　　　3 **mistake** ~ **for** ... = 〜を…とまちがう

ネス湖とネッシー【解決編】　19

Composition

（　　）内のヒントを参考にして、{　　　}の語または語句を並べかえて日本語の意味を表す英文を作ろう。

1. その大地震が起こったとき、あなたは何をしていましたか。（p. 17 読解のポイント）

   { doing / the great earthquake / were / what / when / you } occurred?

   ....

2. 向こうで店員にクレームをつけている男の人はだれですか。（p. 17 読解のポイント）

   { complaining / is / the man / a sales clerk / to / who } over there?

   ....

3. 山道を歩いていると、誰かが助けを求めて叫んでいるのが聞こえた。（p. 17 読解のポイント）

   When I was walking along the mountain path, { crying / for / heard / help / I / someone }.

   ....

Dictation

28~30

音声を聴いて、（　）に書き入れよう。

1. There are (　　　　　　) fish and (　　　　　　) in Loch Ness for a dinosaur to live on.

2. It is (　　　　　　) that many people had seen Nessie (　　　　　) it was reported in 1933.

3. Probably people (　　　　　) a floating log, a (　　　　　) or a seal, and mistook it for Nessie.

20　UNIT 4

Unit 5

魔のバミューダ海域【ミステリー編】

動詞の活用 次の表の空白に書き入れよう。

	原形	過去形	過去分詞形	意味
1	carry			
2	lose			失う
3	go			
4	write			

読解のポイント 【and / but / or】

等位接続詞 and, but, or が出てきたら、次のどれであるか考えよう。

① 語と語を結ぶ　例）Tom **and** I are good friends.

② 句と句を結ぶ（句 = 2つ以上の単語が集まり、まとまった意味をもつもの）

　　例）He came to the party **and** had a good time.

③ 節と節を結ぶ　（節 = 原則として、主語と述語動詞を持ち、文の一部を成す）

　　例）He came to the party **and** we had a good time.

※3つ以上のものを結ぶときには、コンマを使う。
　　A, B and C = A と B と C
　　A, B or C = A か B か C

魔のバミューダ海域【ミステリー編】　21

1 The Bermuda Triangle is a part of the Atlantic Ocean that many people are afraid of. It is between Bermuda, Puerto Rico **and** Florida. Many ships **and** planes have disappeared there, **and** some people believe that some strange power makes it the most dangerous ocean in the world.

2 In 1945, five US Navy planes were flying near Puerto Rico. They talked to their base by radio **and** said they were lost **and** their compasses did not work. They never returned. A rescue plane went to find them, **but** it disappeared too! In 1948, a British airplane carrying 29 people flew from London to Bermuda. Just before it reached Bermuda, it disappeared. In 1950, a ship called the *Sandra* disappeared with 12 people. The plane **and** the ship did not make any radio calls. Many other ships **and** planes were lost in this area.

3 In the 1960's **and** 1970's, books were written about the Bermuda Triangle. They told the stories of the lost planes **and** ships, **and** said that something strange must be happening. There were stories about strange radio calls from the planes **or** ships saying that they saw lights in the sky **or** under the sea. Some of the books said that maybe sea monsters, ghosts, aliens, **or** even strange people living under the sea were the cause. Many people are still afraid to go into the Bermuda Triangle.

4 What is the secret of this mystery?

must ~ = 〜にちがいない (p. 87)

radio calls (...) saying ~ = 〜だと伝える無電通話 (p. 79)

cause = 原因

be afraid to- 不定詞 = 〜するのを怖れている

Listening Comprehension

1〜3の音声を聴いて、本文の内容と合っている英文の番号を○で囲もう。
（1つとは限らない。） 　　1　　2　　3

【ヒント】 2 **go missing** = 行方不明になる

魔のバミューダ海域【ミステリー編】 23

Composition

（　　）内のヒントを参考にして、{　　}の語または語句を並べかえて日本語の意味を表す英文を作ろう。ただし、「または」がついている選択肢については、どちらか1つを選ぼう。

【例】「is または are」→ is か are のうち適切な方を使う。（以下の Unit も同様。）

1. 私の会社と銀行の間にレストランがある。（本文第1段落）

   There { a restaurant / and / between / is または are / my office / the bank }.

   ....

2. トムが昨夜電話をかけてきて、宿題を手伝ってくれと私に頼んだ。（ask ＋人＋ to- 不定詞）（p. 21 読解のポイント）

   Last night Tom { and または but / asked / called / help / me / to } him with his homework.

   ....

3. その男の子はデパートの中で迷子になっていたのだが、親切なおばあさんがその子のために母親を見つけてあげた。（コンマを使うこと。）（p. 21 読解のポイント）

   The little boy { and または but / found / got / in the department store / lost / a kind old lady } his mother for him.

   ....

Dictation

34~36

音声を聴いて、（　　）に書き入れよう。

1. It is (　　　　　) that (　　　　　　) ships nor airplanes got lost in the Bermuda Triangle.

2. There are stories about lost planes and ships (　　　　　) on a (　　　　　) light before they went missing.

3. Many people knew exactly (　　　　　　) the airplanes and ships had (　　　　).

24　UNIT 5

Unit **6**

魔のバミューダ海域【解決編】

動詞の活用　次の表の空白に書き入れよう。

	原形	過去形	過去分詞形	意味
1	read			
2	become			
3	talk			
4	sell			

読解のポイント　【過去形と過去分詞形】

規則活用の一般動詞の過去形と過去分詞形はどちらも -ed で、まぎらわしいので気をつけよう。次のような場合は**過去分詞**であることが多い。

① be 動詞や have (has, had) のすぐあとに続いている

　→　-ed は完了形や受動態で用いられている過去分詞

　　例）He **has finished** the homework.（完了形）(pp. 67–68)

　　　　I **was surprised** at the news.（受動態）(p. 88)

② 名詞のすぐあとに続き、「～される」と訳すと意味が通る

　→　-ed は直前の名詞を修飾する過去分詞 (p. 79)

　　※ 特に、「by ~」という語句を伴うことが多い。

　　　例）This is a picture **taken** by Tom.

魔のバミューダ海域【解決編】　25

37~40

1 The answer is surprising: The Bermuda Triangle is not a very dangerous part of the ocean! Ships and planes have been **lost**, but this area is very busy. Hundreds of ships and planes go through it every day. An area with a lot of traffic will have more accidents than a quiet area. The U.S. Coast Guard and U.S. Navy do not call this area the Bermuda Triangle. They say it's safer than some other areas! So why are people so **scared** of it?

2 The book that really **made** the Bermuda Triangle famous was the best-seller *The Bermuda Triangle* (1974) by Charles Berlitz. Many people **read** the book and **believed** that it really was a dangerous place.

3 But many stories in the book are not true! Some of the ships the book tells about were not even **lost**! They were just a few days late. Some were **lost** very far from the Bermuda Triangle. Many of the airplanes were **lost** in bad weather. The strangest things the book

---

: （コロン）は後に続く節が前の節の内容を説明していることを表す

busy = 忙しい、交通量が多い

more < many【比較級】(p. 90)

U.S. Coast Guard = アメリカ沿岸警備隊
U.S. Navy = アメリカ海軍
call ＋目的語＋補語 = ～を…と呼ぶ (p. 62)
safer < safe【比較級】(p. 90)

Charles Berlitz = チャールズ・ベルリッツ

Some of the ships (which) the book tells about (p. 80)
not even ~ = ～ですらない

strangest < strange【最上級】(p. 90)
the strangest things (that) the book talks about (p. 80)

talks about never **happened**.

4 There were no radio calls about lights in the sky or under the water. Berlitz **made** them up to make the story more interesting. He became rich, and wrote many books. All of his books **told** fantastic stories about mysterious places . . . and most of them **told** stories that were not true!

5 The Bermuda Triangle is really not a mystery. It's just a story **told** to make money by selling books!

make ~ up = 〜をでっちあげる

fantastic = 荒唐無稽な

most = 大部分

Listening Comprehension

1〜3の音声を聴いて、本文の内容と合っている英文の番号を〇で囲もう。
（1つとは限らない。）　　　1　　2　　3

【ヒント】 3 according to ~ = 〜（の言うこと）によれば

Composition

（　）内のヒントを参考にして、{　}の語または語句を並べかえて日本語の意味を表す英文を作ろう。ただし、「または」がついている選択肢については、どちらか1つを選ぼう。

1. 何百人もの人々がその伝記を読んで、彼が本当は偉大な人物だと信じた。（本文第1、第2段落）

   { and / hundreds / of / people / read または reading / the biography } believed that he really was a great man.

   _____

2. チャールズ・ベルリッツによって書かれた本は、多くの人々を怖がらせた。（本文第1段落）

   { by / Charles Berlitz / many people / scared / the book / was written または written }.

   _____

3. 彼はお金を儲けるためにその物語をでっち上げた。（本文第4段落）

   He { made up または was made up / make / money / story / the / to }.

   _____

Dictation

音声を聴いて、（　）に書き入れよう。

1. The Bermuda Triangle is more (　　　　) than any other area of the (　　　　).

2. Charles Berlitz (　　　　) to sell his books, so he wrote about events that didn't (　　　) happen.

3. By (　　　　) fantastic stories about mysterious (　　　　), Charles Berlitz made a lot of money.

Unit 7

ヒマラヤの雪男【ミステリー編】

動詞の活用　次の表の空白に書き入れよう。

	原形	過去形	過去分詞形	意味
1	know			
2	try			
3	send			
4	hide			隠れる、隠す

読解のポイント　【to- 不定詞】

to- 不定詞（to ＋動詞の原形）が出てきたら、次のどれかであることが多い。

① 名詞用法　「～すること」の意味。主語・目的語・補語になる (p. 73)
　　例）She began **to play** the piano.

② 前に名詞が来る　→　形容詞用法　「～するための、～できる」(p. 79)
　　例）I need something **to drink**.

③「～するために、～したので、～するほど」の意味を表す
　　→　副詞用法（句や節を修飾する）(p. 83)
　　例）I went to the library **to borrow** a book.

④ 特定の動詞に対応する　→　動詞＋目的語（人）＋ to- 不定詞
　　例）I asked her **to lend** me her dictionary.

⑤ be ＋ to- 不定詞　→　「～する予定だ、～すべきだ、～できる」などの意味
を表す
　　例）She **was to attend** the ceremony.

ヒマラヤの雪男【ミステリー編】　29

1 The Himalayas are the tallest and most dangerous mountains in the world. They are more than 6,000 meters tall, and many people have died from the cold and thin air, trying **to climb** them. But some people think the Himalayas are hiding a secret.

2 They believe that something strange lives in these mountains. It is an animal called the Yeti. Local people say the Yeti is a 2-meter-tall animal that looks like an ape covered in white hair and walks like a person. Maybe it is a mix of human and ape. Many people say they have seen the Yeti, but no one has ever taken a picture of one. Some people have pictures of footprints, but there is no way **to know** if they are real. The Yeti does not seem **to be** dangerous, but it would be scary **to see** one!

3 Some Buddhist monks say that they have found bones or hair from the Yeti, but they will not usually allow anyone **to study** them. A few of them have let scientists study them.

The scientists found that they were from humans or other ordinary animals.

4 Reports of the Yeti go back hundreds of years, and modern climbers sometimes report seeing it. The Soviet and Chinese armies have sent people **to try to find** it. But no one seems able **to find** out the truth. Are there really ancient ape-men hiding in the Himalayas?

Soviet = ソ連の

army = 陸軍

find out ~ =（努力の末に）〜を探り出す
ancient = 古代の
ape-man = 猿人

Listening Comprehension

1〜3の音声を聴いて、本文の内容と合っている英文の番号を○で囲もう。
（1つとは限らない。）　　　1　　2　　3

Composition

（　）内のヒントを参考にして、{　}の語または語句を並べかえて日本語の意味を表す英文を作ろう。ただし、「または」がついている選択肢については、どちらか1つを選ぼう。

1. 彼が試験に合格したのか知るすべはまったくない。（本文第2段落）

   There is { he / if / know または knowing / no / passed / to / way } the examination.

2. その本はとてもおもしろそうだが、読む時間がない。（本文第2段落）

   The book { be または is / interesting / seems / to / very }, but I don't { have / it / read / time / to }.

3. 先生は学生たちが答えを見つけるためにそのパソコンを使うことを許可した。（本文第3、4段落）

   The teacher { allowed / find または found / his students / the PC / to / to use } the answer.

Dictation

音声を聴いて、（　）に書き入れよう。

1. The Yeti is believed to be an animal that (　　　) like a mix of (　　　) and ape.

2. It is very difficult for many people to (　　　) up the Himalayas because of the (　　　) air.

3. The Soviet and (　　　) armies found out that the Yeti was really an (　　　) ape-man in the Himalayas.

Unit 8

ヒマラヤの雪男【解決編】

動詞の活用　次の表の空白に書き入れよう。

	原形	過去形	過去分詞形	意味
1	think			
2	keep			とっておく
3	give			
4	stand			

読解のポイント　【that】

that が出てきたら、次のどれかであることが多い。

① 代名詞　「あれ（それ）、あの（その）」
　　例）**That** is my pen. / **That** pen is mine.

② 接続詞
　・「～であること」　that- 節の直前に動詞が来ることが多い (p. 75)
　　例）I think **that** he is honest.
　・ある特定の形容詞の後ろにつく (p. 85)
　　例）I'm sure **that** he will come.「～だと確信している」
　・「so [such]~ that- 節」や「so that- 節」の構文 (p. 85)
　　例）The man was so big **that** everyone was surprised.
　　　　I worked hard **so that** I will be rich.

③ 関係代名詞　「～であるところの」 (p. 80)
　　例）The man **that** I met at the party was very funny.

ヒマラヤの雪男【解決編】　33

1 Many people said **that** they had found hair, bones or skin from a dead Yeti. But every time these were tested by scientists, they were found to be from goats or other normal animals. It seemed there was nothing to prove **that** the Yeti was real.

2 In 2013, scientists were able to study two animal skins **that** were said to be from Yetis. One of them was given by the family of a hunter who had killed it 40 years before. He thought the animal was so strange **that** he kept the skin.

3 The scientists looked at DNA from the skins. The results were a surprise. The skins came from bears! There are bears in the Himalayas, but they are brown and seldom stand up. But this was not an ordinary bear. The DNA matched a type of polar bear **that** has not been in the Himalayas for 40,000 years! It could walk on two legs some of the time.

4 The scientists do not think **that** these polar bears have lived in the Himalayas for all this time. They think they mixed with other bears in the area before they died out. The mixed bears can probably stand up and probably have white fur, just like the Yeti. People who saw a big white animal standing up in a snowstorm became very frightened, and the story of the Yeti was born.

5 It seems **that** the Yeti stories were half-true! The Yeti is real . . . it's just not an ape-man.

for all this time = これまでの間ずっと
mix = 交配する

die out = 死に絶える

fur = 毛皮

snowstorm = 吹雪
frighten = 怖がらせる（scareとほぼ同義）

Listening Comprehension

1〜3の音声を聴いて、本文の内容と合っている英文の番号を○で囲もう。
（1つとは限らない。）　　　1　　2　　3

【ヒント】 3 **rarely** =めったに〜ない

Composition

（　　）内のヒントを参考にして、{　　}の語または語句を並べかえて日本語の意味を表す英文を作ろう。ただし、「または」がついている選択肢については、どちらか1つを選ぼう。

1. 彼が有罪だと証明するものは何ひとつ見つからなかった。（本文第1段落）

   { found または didn't find / I / nothing / prove / that / to } he was guilty.

   ....

2. ヒマラヤ山脈の風景がとても美しいと思ったので、それを写真に撮った。（本文第2段落）

   I thought { of the Himalayas / so beautiful / the landscape / that / that / is または was } I took a picture of it.

   ....

3. 先生が後ろに立っているのを目にした学生たちはおしゃべりをやめた。（本文第4段落）

   The students { behind them / saw / standing または stood / stopped / the teacher / who } talking.

   ....

Dictation

55~57

音声を聴いて、（　）に書き入れよう。

1. It (　　　　　) that the Yeti is some (　　　　　) of gorilla.
2. The DNA from the Yeti (　　　　　) (　　　　　) a type of polar bear.
3. The (　　　　　) bears in the Himalayas rarely stand on two (　　　　　).

36　UNIT 8

消えた乗組員の謎【ミステリー編】

動詞の活用　次の表の空白に書き入れよう。

	原形	過去形	過去分詞形	意味
1	leave			出発する
2	take			連れて行く
3	drink			
4	fall			落ちる、落とす

読解のポイント　【節のつなげかた】

節のつなげ方には2種類ある。

① **and, but, or, so**（それで）, **for**（というのも）が用いられている
　→　2つの節は対等な関係にある。
　　　例）It rained all day **and** we stayed home.

② **that**（〜ということ）, **if**（もし〜ならば）, **as**（〜なので、〜とき）, **when**（〜とき）, **though [although]**（〜だけれども）が用いられている
　→　これらの接続詞で導かれる節（従属節）は主節に付属する意味合いをもつ
　　　例）

　　　　　従属節　　　　　　　　　　　主節
　　　　As it rained all day,　　　we stayed home.

消えた乗組員の謎【ミステリー編】　37

1 In 1872, a ship named *Mary Celeste* left New York carrying alcohol to Italy. A few days later a ship named *Dei Gratia* found the *Mary Celeste* in the middle of the ocean. There was no one on the ship. It had no damage, **and** the cargo was still there. The small lifeboat was gone. Why had the sailors left the ship? There was no reason for them to leave in a small boat in the middle of the ocean! The weather was bad, **so** it is likely that they died before reaching land. Sailors from the *Dei Gratia* took the *Mary Celeste* to Gibraltar. No one ever learned what happened to the *Mary Celeste* sailors.

2 In 1883 a newspaper told the story again. It said that the ship's oven was still warm, **and** plates of food were sitting on the table. Papers were on the captain's desk. A bottle of ink was sitting open, but had not spilled. Everything was normal. The ship was in perfect condition . . . **but** the crew were gone.

3 In 1884, Arthur Conan Doyle, who wrote the *Sherlock Holmes* series, wrote a story about the *Mary Celeste*. In this story, the sailors were all murdered by another sailor. People did not think it was true, **but** it made the mystery more famous.

murder = 殺す

4 There are ideas about what happened. Some people think **that** sea monsters or pirates or even aliens took the sailors! Some think **that** one sailor went crazy and killed everyone, or **that** they drank too much alcohol and fell off the ship.

pirate = 海賊
some think that- 節 = 〜だと考える人々もいる
go crazy = 発狂する

5 So what really happened?

so = それでは

Listening Comprehension

1〜3の音声を聴いて、本文の内容と合っている英文の番号を○で囲もう。
（1つとは限らない。）　　　1　　2　　3

Composition

（　）内のヒントを参考にして、｛　｝の語または語句を並べかえて日本語の意味を表す英文を作ろう。ただし、「または」がついている選択肢については、どちらか1つを選ぼう。

1. その列車は多くの人を載せて下関から博多へと出発した。（本文第1段落）

   The train { carry または carrying / to Hakata / left / many / people / Shimonoseki }.

   ....

2. もし雨が降り出したならば、学生たちはおそらく試合を中止するだろう。（コンマを使うこと）（本文第1段落）

   { as または if / begins / to rain / it / it is / likely } that the students will call off the game.

   ....

3. 私はそのニュースを本当だとは思わなかったが、興味を持った。（コンマを使うこと。）（本文第3段落）

   I didn't { but または that / it / made / the news / think / was true } me curious.

   ....

Dictation

音声を聴いて、（　）に書き入れよう。

1. It is believed that the sailors were all (　　　　) by (　　　　) sailor.
2. Although the *Mary Celeste* was in good (　　　　), the crew and the life boat were (　　　　).
3. The (　　　　) of the *Mary Celeste* was made more (　　　　) by a story written by Conan Doyle.

Unit 10

消えた乗組員の謎【解決編】

動詞の活用 次の表の空白に書き入れよう。

	原形	過去形	過去分詞形	意味
1	leak			漏れる
2	reach			到着する
3	light			点火する
4	burn			燃える、燃やす

読解のポイント 【助動詞の過去形】

助動詞の過去形が出てきたら、次のどれかであることが多い。

① that- 節や if- 節などの中にあり、その前に said, thought などの動詞がある

→ 時制の一致

例）I thought that he **would** come.

② if などがある → 仮定法 (p. 91)

例）If it were fine today, I **would** go fishing.

③ それ以外

(1) ていねいさを表したり、断定を避ける

"Shall we go fishing?" "That would be nice."

(2) 現在や過去の事柄についての推測を表す

She left an hour ago. She would be home now.

※過去の事柄の場合は、would have ＋ 過去分詞が用いられることが多い（本文 14, 25 行目参照）。

消えた乗組員の謎【解決編】 41

1 To begin with, the famous newspaper story was not accurate. The writer did not read the original report. There was no warm oven, food sitting on tables, or ink bottles. There was a lot of seawater in the ship because the hatches of the cargo area were open. Maps and navigation tools were gone. The sailors left the ship with the things they needed to reach land. But why?

2 The original report said that nine of the alcohol barrels were empty. They were not the right kind of barrels to hold alcohol. They had leaked! Over 900 liters of alcohol had leaked out. The fumes **would** have filled the ship. There were over 1,000 barrels, so it was hard to find the bad ones. The sailors probably opened the hatches to get the fumes out. They may have been afraid the ship **would** explode, so they left in the small lifeboat.

3 Maybe an explosion did happen. In 2006,

---

to begin with = まず最初に【成句】
accurate = 正確な
original = 元々の

hatch = 昇降口
navigation tool = 航海用具

barrel = 樽（たる）
right = 正しい
liter = リットル
fume = 煙・ガス・蒸気
1,000 = one thousand

get ~ out = ～を外に出す
they may have been afraid that-節 = 彼らは～だと怖れたのかもしれない (p. 86)
explode = 爆発する

did happen = happened【強調】

a professor filled a model of the cargo area with alcohol fumes. When he lit a fire there was a loud explosion big enough to make people think wood **would** have caught fire. But an alcohol explosion is not so hot, and is over quickly. The model was not damaged. Even paper did not burn!

4 If such an explosion had happened on the ship, the sailors **might** have panicked and left. If the sailors had stayed on the ship, they **would** probably have lived.

5 We cannot know for sure why the sailors left the *Mary Celeste*. But it is very likely that they left the ship because of alcohol fumes and fear of an explosion, not aliens or sea monsters or murder!

professor = 教授
model = 模型
cargo area = 貨物区画

big enough to- 不定詞 = 〜するほど大きな (p. 83)

be over = 終わる

panic = 恐慌をきたす

for sure = 確実に【成句】

because of 〜 = 〜のせいで【成句】
fear = 恐れ

Listening Comprehension

1〜3の音声を聴いて、本文の内容と合っている英文の番号を○で囲もう。
（1つとは限らない。）　　　1　　2　　3

Composition

（　）内のヒントを参考にして、{　}の語または語句を並べかえて日本語の意味を表す英文を作ろう。ただし、「または」がついている選択肢については、どちらか1つを選ぼう。

1. ニュースによれば、その宇宙船は1週間以内に火星にたどり着くだろうとのことだった。（本文第1、2段落）
   The { Mars / news / reach / said / will または would / that / the spaceship } within a week.

   ....

2. もし屋根が雨漏りしていなければ、私たちは小屋から出て行かないだろうに。（コンマを使うこと）(p. 91)
   If { leaking / leave / might または would / not / the roof / we / weren't } the hut.

   ....

3. もし屋根が雨漏りしていなかったならば、私たちはその小屋で一夜を明かしたかもしれなかった。（コンマを使うこと）(p. 91)
   We { had / have / if / in the hut / might または would / spent the night / the roof } not leaked.

   ....

Dictation

音声を聴いて、（　）に書き入れよう。

1. The (　　　) fumes (　　　) and sank the ship.
2. If the sailors had not (　　　), they would have been burnt to (　　　).
3. Nobody knows what really (　　　) to the (　　　).

44　UNIT 10

Unit 11

ミイラの呪い【ミステリー編】

動詞の活用　次の表の空白に書き入れよう。

	原形	過去形	過去分詞形	意味
1	discover			
2	pay			
3	show			
4	study			

読解のポイント　【関係詞節】

who (whom) や which, that, what などの関係詞節が文中に出てきたら、その節がどこで終わっているかを見きわめよう。関係詞節の次には動詞が来ることが多い。(p. 80)

例）　The man **who made this discovery** became very rich.
　　　　主語　　　　　　　　　　　　　　述語動詞

　　　The wine **which I bought yesterday** was very expensive.
　　　　主語　　　　　　　　　　　　　　述語動詞

　　　What surprised me was his good score.
　　　　主語　　　　　　述語動詞

ミイラの呪い【ミステリー編】　45

1 In 1922 the 3,000-year-old tomb of King Tutankhamun of Egypt was discovered. It was opened by British archaeologist Howard Carter. He had been looking for the tomb for over 15 years. Lord Carnarvon, the man **who** paid for the search, asked him if he could see anything when he opened the door. Carter said, "Yes, wonderful things."

2 Tutankhamun's tomb had a lot of gold and other treasures, and soon became famous around the world. Tutankhamun's mummy and treasure were soon studied and shown in museums in England.

3 But there was also danger. Newspapers wrote stories about a curse on the tomb. They said that anyone **who** opened the tomb would die. Soon people connected with the tomb began to die. An Egyptian prince **who** visited the tomb was killed by his wife the next month. The doctor **who** x-rayed Tutankhamun's mummy died a few days later of a fever.

---

tomb = 墓所

Tutankhamun = ツタンカーメン

archaeologist = 考古学者

look for ~ = ~をさがす

Lord Carnarvon = カルナルヴォン卿

treasure = 宝物

mummy = ミイラ

curse = 呪い

(be) connected with [to] ~ = ~と関係がある

X-ray ~ = ~のレントゲン写真を撮る
die of ~ = ~で死ぬ（直接的な原因）
fever = 高熱

46　UNIT 11

4 Carter's friend, George Gould, became sick and died soon after seeing the mummy. Within a year, Lord Carnarvon was dead from an infection, and his brother died a year later. Carter's assistant killed himself in 1928 and another member of his team died of poison in 1929.

5 Of the 44 people **who** were there when the tomb was opened, 13 died in the next twenty years. Even Carter's parrot was killed by a cobra the day he opened the tomb!

6 Was King Tutankhamun's curse real?

George Gould = ジョージ・グールド

within ~ = ～以内に

infection = 感染

poison = 毒

of the 44 people = 44人の人々のうちで

parrot = オウム

(on) the day (when) he opened the tomb = 彼が墓所を開いた日に (p. 82)

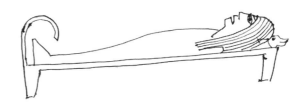

Listening Comprehension

1～3の音声を聴いて、本文の内容と合っている英文の番号を○で囲もう。
（1つとは限らない。）　　　1　　2　　3

【ヒント】 1 **financial** = 金銭上の

Composition

（　）内のヒントを参考にして、{　}の語または語句を並べかえて日本語の意味を表す英文を作ろう。ただし、「または」がついている選択肢については、どちらか1つを選ぼう。

1. カロリーを摂取し過ぎる人はしばしば体重が増えます。(p. 45 読解のポイント)
   { too many calories / people / often / put on / take in / weight / who または whom }.

2. 昨日食べたお寿司はとてもおいしかった。(p. 45 読解のポイント)
   { ate / I / the sushi / was / which または whom / very good / yesterday }.

3. 試合中にぎっくり腰になった選手はあなたですか。(get a slipped disc) (p. 45 読解のポイント)
   Are { got a slipped disc / during / the player / the game / who または whose / you }?

Dictation

音声を聴いて、(　)に書き入れよう。

1. Howard Carter was a financial (　　　) of the group that (　　　) the tomb of King Tutankhamun.
2. Lord Carnarvon was (　　　) in a traffic (　　　) in Egypt.
3. Carter's (　　　) died 6 years after the (　　　) was opened.

Unit 12

ミイラの呪い【解決編】

動詞の活用　次の表の空白に書き入れよう。

	原形	過去形	過去分詞形	意味
1	steal			
2	open			開ける
3	die			
4	connect			関係させる、つなげる

読解のポイント　【前置詞句】

前置詞句（前置詞＋名詞）については、次の点に気をつけよう。

① 前置詞句が直前の名詞を修飾する場合 (p. 78)

　例）Look at the cat **on the roof**.

　　　（on the roof は the cat を修飾している。「屋根の上のネコ」）

② 前置詞句がある特定の語と結びついている場合

　例）The poor elephant **died from hunger**.

　　　（die from ~ = ～が原因で死ぬ〈間接的な原因〉）

　　This cord is **connected to that machine**.

　　（connect ~ to ... = ～を…につなぐ）

ミイラの呪い【解決編】　49

1 Egyptian tombs often had curses written on the doors to keep away people who might steal the gold and other valuable things. But the curse **on King Tut's tomb** is only written about in newspaper stories. Newspaper stories **at that time** often had very exciting details... but often these were not true. All **of the things from the tomb** are in museums, but nothing has a curse written on it. The newspaper writers probably wrote about the curse so more people would read their stories!

2 What about all the people who died after the tomb was opened? Some deaths **in the group** were not surprising. Some **of the people, including Lord Carnarvon**, were already in bad health or were old. Some died in accidents or **from being sick**. Safety and medical care was very bad in Egypt then, and many people died **from accidents** or disease. Some **of the people** were not closely

---

★前置詞のうち、「読解のポイント」①②に該当するもののみ太字にしてある。
Egyptian < Egypt
keep away = 近寄らせない

valuable = 高価な

Tut = Tutankhamun
write about ~ = 〜について書く

details【複数形】= 詳細

so (that) 主語 + 述語動詞 = 〜が…するように → (p. 85)

what about ~ ? = 〜はどうなのか？

including ~ = 〜を含めて【前置詞】

safety and medical care = 治安と医療

disease = 病気
be closely connected = 密接な関係がある

connected **to Carter**, or died 10 years later! In 2002 *BMJ*, a British medical journal, looked at the case. They found that the number **of people in the group** who died in the next twenty years was *lower* than average for a group **in that area at that time**!

medical journal = 医学雑誌

case = 事件

lower 強調のため斜字体にしてある

Listening Comprehension

1～3の音声を聴いて、本文の内容と合っている英文の番号を〇で囲もう。
（1つとは限らない。）　　　1　　　2　　　3

【ヒント】　2 **exaggerated** = 誇張された／**attract** = ひきつける
　　　　　3 **evidence** = 証拠

ミイラの呪い【解決編】　51

Composition

（　）内のヒントを参考にして、｛　｝の語または語句を並べかえて日本語の意味を表す英文を作ろう。ただし、「または」がついている選択肢については、どちらか1つを選ぼう。

1. 豪華なドレスを着ているあの女性は私の上司です。(p. 49 読解のポイント)
   { the / dress / gorgeous / for または in / is / that / woman } my boss.

2. 大統領は通り過ぎずに私の前で止まった。(p. 49 読解のポイント)
   The { before または in front / instead of / of me / stopped / president / walking } past.

3. 彼女が薬指にはめている指輪のダイヤを見てください。(p. 49 読解のポイント)
   { at または for / look / on / on her third finger / the diamond / the ring }.

Dictation

音声を聴いて、（　）に書き入れよう。

1. All of the Egyptian tombs, (　　　　) King Tutankhamun's, had curses written on the (　　　　).
2. The (　　　　) writers at the time wrote exaggerated stories about the curse to attract public (　　　　).
3. The (　　　　) medical journal (　　　　) no evidence about King Tutankhamun's curse.

Unit 13

ディアトロフ峠殺人事件【Part 1】

動詞の活用　次の表の空白に書き入れよう。

	原形	過去形	過去分詞形	意味
1	explain			説明する
2	plan			
3	return			戻る
4	tear			裂く、破る

読解のポイント　【コンマ】

次のようなコンマの用法には特に注意しよう。

① and を用いずに 2 つまたはそれ以上の形容詞を並べる

　　例）a big, beautiful flower (= a big and beautiful flower)

② and や or を用いて 3 つ以上の語（語句）を並列する

　「A, B そして（または）C」

　　例）He went out, came back, took the car key and went out again.

③〈同格〉を表す　「〜、すなわち…」

　　例）Arthur Conan Doyle, the author of the *Sherlock Holmes* series, was
　　　　born in 1859.

④ 挿入句・節の前後

　　例）Arthur Conan Doyle, who wrote the *Sherlock Holmes* series, was
　　　　born in 1859.

ディアトロフ峠殺人事件【Part 1】　53

1 We have talked about many mysteries in this book. We have shown that most of them can be explained. But there are some that are not explained. They are "real" mysteries. One of these is the Dyatlov Pass Mystery.

2 In January 1959, a group of university friends in Sverdlovsk, Russia, went on a ski trek. They wanted to reach a mountain called Otorten. The land around Otorten is very rough, and in winter it is very cold. It was –2℃ on the day they left! The group were good skiers and often went on long ski trips together. They planned to travel 250 km in 15 days. They left on January 27th.

3 When the group did not return after 20 days, the Soviet Army began looking for them with helicopters. They found them very quickly in the Dyatlov Pass, a low place between two high mountains. It was near the beginning of their trip. They had died very soon after they started. People often die in

some = some mysteries

pass = 峠

Sverdlovsk = スヴェルドロフスク（現エカチェリンブルグ。ロシア共和国ウラル地方中部の同名州の州都）
trek = （特に徒歩の）旅行

–2℃ = minus two degrees Celsius [Centigrade]
on the day (when) the left (p. 82)
go on a trip = 旅行に出かける

bad weather in Russia. But this was not a normal accident. Something very strange had happened.

4 Their tent was torn apart. Their clothing, food and equipment were scattered around. Two bodies were near the tent, and the other seven were further away. None of them had their coats on! Some had no shoes, and no gloves. Footprints in the snow showed that they had run from the tent in panic and died from the cold. But why?

tear ~ apart = 引き裂く
clothing = 衣類
equipment = 用具
scatter = ばらまく

further < far = 遠くに

coat = 上着
on = 身に着けて【副詞】

in panic = あわてふためいて

Listening Comprehension

1〜3の音声を聴いて、本文の内容と合っている英文の番号を○で囲もう。
（1つとは限らない。）　　　1　　2　　3

【ヒント】 3 incident = できごと

Composition

（　　）内のヒントを参考にして、{　　}の語または語句を並べかえて日本語の意味を表す英文を作ろう。ただし、「または」がついている選択肢については、どちらか1つを選ぼう。必ずコンマを使うこと。

1. チーズバーガーとフライドポテト、バニラシェイクをください。（p. 53　読解のポイント）

   { a cheeseburger / a vanilla shake / and または but / French fries / have / I'll }, please.

   ....

2. 有名な作家を父親にもつユリは大学で英文学を学んでいる。（p. 53　読解のポイント）

   Yuri, { a famous writer / at college / English literature / father / is / is studying / who または whose }.

   ....

3. こちらがブルース・リーさん、香港からきた交換留学生です。（p. 53　読解のポイント）

   { an / Hong Kong / exchange / from / is または are / Mr. Bruce Lee / student / this }.

   ....

Dictation

90~92

音声を聴いて、（　）に書き入れよう。

1. The (　　　　　) had been on ski trips (　　　　　) before.

2. The Soviet Army found two (　　　　　) near the top of Mt. Otorten and couldn't find the others (　　　　　).

3. It was near the (　　　　　) of the trip that they (　　　　　) in the mysterious incident.

56　UNIT 13

Unit 14

ディアトロフ峠殺人事件【Part 2】

動詞の活用 次の表の空白に書き入れよう。

	原形	過去形	過去分詞形	意味
1	break			
2	hit			
3	panic			〜に恐慌を起こさせる
4	throw			

読解のポイント 【同じ形の名詞と動詞】

名詞と動詞、名詞と形容詞が同じ形である単語が、英語にはたくさんある。**動詞**の場合には -ed がついていることが多い。

例） **snow** 雪【名詞】、雪が降る【動詞】

water 水【名詞】、（植物に）水をやる【動詞】

button ボタン【名詞】、ボタンをはめる【動詞】

cold 寒さ・風邪【名詞】、寒い【形容詞】

bite 噛み傷【名詞】、噛む【動詞】

force 力・軍隊【名詞】、無理やり〜させる【動詞】

print 跡【名詞】、（型を）押しつける、印刷する【動詞】

damage 損害【名詞】、損害を与える【動詞】

ディアトロフ峠殺人事件【Part 2】 57

[1] No one knows why they ran from their tent. Film from their camera showed a normal happy trip. The last pictures showed the weather getting bad, and the group making a camp. Nothing looked strange. But later they ran out into a –5℃ snowstorm without their shoes or coats. Then it became stranger. Doctors said that three of them had not died from the **cold**. They had been killed by a strong **force** that broke their bones! It looked like they had been hit by a speeding car.

[2] Maybe wild animals had attacked their tent, panicking them. There are bears in these mountains, but there were no **bites** or **cuts** on the bodies, and no animal **prints** in the snow.

[3] Maybe an avalanche had torn their tent apart and thrown three of them into trees. But the helicopter pilot saw no signs of an avalanche, and the tent was not covered by

look like ~ = ～であるように見える、思われる【like は接続詞扱い】
speed = 高速で走る

avalance = なだれ

sign = しるし、徴候、気配
be covered by [with] ~ = ～でおおわれている

snow. The group knew all about camping in winter. They knew that they could not run faster than an avalanche, and that it is safest to stay together.

safest < safe【最上級】(p. 90)

4 The Soviet Army sometimes tested bombs and guns in this area, so maybe they were killed by accident. But the Army would not do tests in bad weather, and there were no signs of tests in the area.

bomb = 爆弾

by accident = 偶然に、誤って

5 The Dyatlov Pass Mystery is one of the strangest and scariest true stories in the world. Maybe no one will ever know what really happened.

scariest < scary

 Listening Comprehension

1～3の音声を聴いて、本文の内容と合っている英文の番号を○で囲もう。
（1つとは限らない。）　　　1　　2　　3

【ヒント】2 **possibility** = 可能性

ディアトロフ峠殺人事件【Part 2】　59

Composition

本文を参考にして、{　}の単語または語句を並べかえて日本語の意味を表す英文を作ろう。ただし、「または」がついている選択肢については、どちらか1つを選ぼう。

1. ハチは毎日渋谷駅で主人の帰りを待ちました。(p. 57 読解のポイント)
   Hachi { at / for /his / master's / return または returned / waited } Shibuya Station every day.

   ....

2. 私は母にメールを送り、10万円振り込んでくれと頼んだ。(p. 57 読解のポイント)
   I { and / asked / e-mail または e-mailed / her / my mother / to } transfer 100,000 yen to my account.

   ....

3. 迷惑メールにうんざりして、メールアドレスを変更した。(p. 57 読解のポイント)
   I { and / changed / got / e-mail または e-mailed / junk / sick of } my e-mail address.

   ....

Dictation

音声を聴いて、(　)に書き入れよう。

1. Three of the group (　　　　) to death and the others were killed by (　　　　) animals in the mountains.

2. There is a strong possibility that (　　　　) military training or bears in the mountains were the (　　　　) of their death.

3. (　　　　) has ever found what happened to the (　　　　) in the Dyatlov Pass on that day.

60　UNIT 14

巻末付録 1

文法解説

文法解説 I

5 文型

英文の基本的な構造は《主語＋述語動詞》である。その後にどんな文の要素が続くかによって、5つの文型に分かれる。

第1文型　SV《主語＋述語動詞》（動詞は自動詞）
　例）I get up at 7 every morning.　私は毎朝7時に起きます。
　　　S V

第2文型　SVC《主語＋述語動詞＋補語》（動詞は自動詞）
　例）I am a student.　私は学生です。
　　　S V　　C

第3文型　SVO《主語＋述語動詞＋目的語》（動詞は他動詞）
　例）I like apples.　私はりんごが好きだ。
　　　S V　　O

第4文型　SVOO《主語＋述語動詞＋間接目的語＋直接目的語》（動詞は他動詞）
　例）He gave me some money.　彼は私にいくらかのお金をくれた。
　　　S　　V　O　　　　O

第5文型　SVOC《主語＋述語動詞＋目的語＋補語》（動詞は他動詞）
　例）Nessie made the lake famous.　ネッシーがその湖を有名にした。
　　　　S　　V　　O　　C

※ 他動詞と自動詞のちがい
　　他動詞　transitive verb (vt.)　　= 目的語をとる
　　自動詞　intransitive verb (vi.)　= 目的語をとらない

62　文法解説

文法解説 II

時の表し方

言語で、〈現在〉や〈過去〉、〈未来〉といった〈時間の状態〉を表すことを時制という。
時制の違いは**動詞**の形を変えることで表す。

主な時制

① 現在形

例）I study English every day.　私は英語を毎日勉強する。

② 過去形

例）I studied English yesterday.　私は英語を昨日勉強した。

③ 未来形

例）It will rain tomorrow.　明日雨が降るだろう。

④ 現在完了形

例）I have finished my homework.　宿題を終えてしまった。

⑤ 過去完了形

例）I had finished my homework when he came.

彼が来たとき、私はすでに宿題を終えていた。

⑥ 未来完了形

例）I will have finished my homework by tomorrow.

私は明日には宿題を終えているだろう。

II 時の表し方　63

II-1 時の表し方 ① 現在形

① 動詞の現在形は〈現在の状態〉や〈反復動作や習慣〉などを表す。
② 動詞の現在形のつくりかた　　原則として、原形または原形＋(e)s
　※ be 動詞については下の表参照。have → has（主語 3 人称単数の場合）

現在形が表す主な意味

〈現在の状態〉　　例）She loves pasta.　彼女はパスタが好きだ。

〈現在の反復動作や習慣〉

　　例）I always go to bed late at night.　私は寝るのがいつも遅い。

〈一般的な事実や真理〉

　　例）The sun rises in the east.　太陽は東から昇る。

〈変わることのない状況や、定期的に行われたり起きること〉

　　例）We have a lot of rain in June.　6 月にはたくさん雨が降る。

※現在形で未来のできごとを表すこともある。(p. 66)

主語の人称と動詞の現在形

人称	主語になる語	be 動詞の形	一般動詞
1 人称（話し手）単数	I	am 例）I am a student.	原形のまま 例）I play baseball.
1 人称（話し手）複数	we	are 例）We are students.	原形のまま 例）We play baseball.
2 人称（聞き手）単数・複数	you	are 例）You are a student.	原形のまま 例）You play baseball.
3 人称（その他）単数	he, she, it など	is 例）He is a student.	原形の語尾に s 例）He plays baseball.
3 人称（その他）複数	they など	are 例）They are students.	原形のまま 例）They play baseball.

※語尾の -s の特殊なつけかた

　① [s, z, ʃ, tʃ, dʒ] の発音で終わる動詞 → 語尾に es をつける。例）wash → washes

　② 子音＋y で終わる動詞 → 語尾の y を i に変えて es をつける。

　　　例）study → studies

【練習】正しいものを○で囲もう。

1. My little sister (cry / cries) every night.
2. Tom and Jane (study / studies) English every day.
3. She (watch / watches) TV late at night.

64　文法解説

II-2　時の表し方 ②　過去形

① 動詞の過去形は、〈現在から切り離された過去のある時点〉の事柄を表すのに使われる。

※ 時間の長短にかかわらず、現在とは切り離されている。

　　例）I got up 1 minute ago.　私は1分前に起きた。

（過去）　　　起きた　　　　　　　　　　　　　　　　　　　　　　　　　　（未来）

　　　　　　　　1分前　　　　現在

② 過去形のつくりかた

(1) 規則動詞　——原形の語尾に -ed をつける

(2) 不規則動詞——変化のしかたが不規則 (pp. 94–95)

　　例）be 動詞の過去形は　is / am　→　was,　are　→　were

過去形が表す主な意味

〈過去の動作や状態〉

　　例）He played baseball last Sunday.　彼は先週の日曜日に野球をした。

〈過去に反復して行われた動作や習慣〉

　　例）I studied English every day in my high school days.

　　　　高校生のころ私は毎日英語を勉強していた。

規則動詞の過去形のつくりかた　（不規則動詞の活用表は pp. 94–95 参照）

(1) 原則的に、原形の語尾に -ed をつける　　例）walk → walked

(2) e で終わる動詞　→　-d だけつける　　例）live → lived

(3) 子音 + y で終わる動詞　→　y を i に変えて ed をつける　　例）study → studied

(4) 短母音 + 子音で終わる動詞　→　子音を重ねて ed をつける　　例）stop → stopped

※ -ed の発音には以下のようなものがある

[t]	[id]	[d]
passed / worked など	waited / needed など	opened / played など

【練習】正しいものを○で囲もう。

1. I wanted to be a teacher when I (was / were) a boy.

2. I always get up when the sun (rises / rose).

3. He (wears / wore) brown shoes when I met him.

II 時の表し方　65

II–3　時の表し方 ③　未来の表現

〈未来のできごとについての予測〉を表す主なやり方は次の2つである。
① will ＋ 動詞の原形
② be going to ＋ 動詞の原形

「will ＋ 動詞の原形」が表す主な意味

〈単純未来〉話し手や主語の意図に関係なく、〈未来に起こると予測されること〉を表す

例）I will be 18 next birthday.　次の誕生日には18才になります。

〈意志未来〉話し手の〈意志〉を表す

例）I will study hard to pass the exam.
　　　試験に合格するために一生懸命勉強するつもりだ。

「be going to ＋ 動詞の原形」が表す主な意味

主に、話者にとって〈未来にするつもりでいたこと〉や〈起こりそうだと思っていること〉を表すのに使う。

〈近い未来の予測〉

例）It's going to rain.　雨が降りそうだ。（雨が降り出しそうな空模様）

〈前から持っていた意図〉

例）Are you going to go fishing next Sunday?　日曜日に釣りに行くつもりですか。

※ 現在形や進行形を使って〈未来〉を表すこともある。

例）Our train leaves at 6 this evening.　列車は夕方の6時に出ます。
　　　We are leaving tomorrow.　私たちは明日出発します。

【練習】正しいものを○で囲もう。

1. What (are / will) you going to be when you grow up?
2. There (is going / will) be a big sports event in Yamaguchi next year.
3. (Is / Will) it be fine next Sunday ?

66　文法解説

II–4　時の表し方 ④　現在完了形

① 現在完了形は、物事の〈完了・結果〉・〈経験〉・〈継続〉など、過去から現在にわたっ
て関係しているできごとについて述べる場合に用いる。

　　例）I have lost my pen.　私はペンをなくした。

（過去）　　　なくした　　　　　　　　今もなくしたまま　　　　　　（未来）

　　　　　　　過去のある時点　　　　　　　　現在

　　※ 過去形　I lost my pen yesterday.　私は昨日ペンをなくした。

　　　　　　　（現在の状況については言及していない）

② 現在完了形のつくりかた

　have ＋ 過去分詞（動詞の原形 ＋ -ed）※不規則動詞については pp. 94–95 参照

現在完了形が表す主な意味

〈完了・結果〉ちょうど今終わったこと、その結果として現在起こった（起こっている）
こと

　　例）He has changed.　彼は変わってしまった。

〈経験〉話し手にとっての現在までの経験

　　例）I have visited New York twice.

　　　　　　私は（今までに）ニューヨークを2度訪れたことがある。

〈経験〉現在まで続いてきたこと、やってきたこと

　　例）He has been absent from school for 3 days.

　　　　　　彼は（今まで）学校を3日間欠席している。

現在完了形の疑問文と否定文のつくりかた

　　例）I have lost my pen.

　　　→　【否定文】Have you lost your pen?

　　　　　【疑問文】I haven't lost my pen.

【練習】正しいものを○で囲もう。

1.　He (has finished / have finished) reading the book.

2.　Have you ever (saw / seen) a polar bear?

3.　Three weeks (have passed / passed) since I saw him at the party.

II 時の表し方　67

II-5 時の表し方 ⑤ 過去完了形

過去完了形（had ＋過去分詞）は、過去のある時点の物事がそれ以前にあった物事と関係していることを表す。

① 過去のある時点（過去形で表す）における物事の〈完了〉、〈結果〉、〈経験〉、〈継続〉を表す
② 過去のある時点より以前に起きたことについて述べる（大過去）

過去完了形が表す主な意味

〈完了・結果〉過去のある時点で終わったこと、その結果としてその時起こったこと

例）When I met him, he had changed.

　　私が彼に会ったとき、彼は変わってしまっていた。

〈経験〉話し手にとっての過去のある時点までの経験

例）I had seen the picture before then.

　　私はその映画を（その時までに）見たことがあった。

〈継続〉過去のある時点まで続いてきた、やってきたこと

例）I had studied English for 6 years before I entered the university.

　　大学に入学する前まで、私は英語を6年間学んできていた。

〈大過去〉2つの出来事の時間的な前後関係

例）He got a job as a teacher. He had graduated from the university ten years before.

　　彼は教師の仕事を得た。彼はその10年前に大学を卒業していた。

※ 過去完了形を用いなくても、物事の前後関係がはっきりわかる場合は、**過去形**が用いられる。

例）He wrote the letter and posted it.

　　彼は手紙を書き、それを投函した。（had written は不可）

〰〰〰〰〰〰〰〰〰〰〰〰〰〰〰〰〰〰〰〰〰〰〰〰〰〰〰〰

【練習】正しいものを○で囲もう。

1. The train (has already left / had already left) when I arrived at the station.

2. I gave him a book which I (bought / had bought) three days before.

3. I (had gone / went) to the library and borrowed 3 books yesterday.

68　文法解説

II-6 時の表し方 ⑥ 未来完了形

未来完了（will [shall] have + 過去分詞）は、未来のある時点までの〈完了〉、〈結果〉、〈継続〉、〈経験〉を表す。

未来完了が表す主な意味

〈完了・結果〉
　例）I will have finished my work by tomorrow.
　　　　明日までに仕事を終わらせてしまっているだろう。

〈経験〉
　例）By the time I take the exam, I will have read the textbook more than ten times.
　　　　試験を受けるときまでに教科書を10回以上は読んでいることだろう。

〈継続〉
　例）I will have worked for this company for ten years next month.
　　　　来月にはこの会社に勤めて10年になります。

【練習】正しいものを◯で囲もう。
1. We (have been / will have been) friends since childhood
2. I (have written / will have written) my letter before I go to bed.
3. I (have written / had written) my letter by yesterday morning.

II–7　時の表し方 ⑦　進行形

進行形（be 動詞＋ ~ing）はある特定の時点における〈行動や状態の継続・進行〉を表す。

主な進行形
① 現在進行形　「am / are / is ＋ ~ing」
② 過去進行形　「was / were ＋ ~ing」
③ 未来進行形　「will [shall] be ＋ ~ing」
④ 現在完了進行形　「have [has] been ＋ ~ing」
⑤ 過去完了進行形　「had been ＋ ~ing」

動詞の ~ing 形のつくりかた

・多くの動詞にはそのまま ing をつける。　例）play → play<u>ing</u>、walk → walk<u>ing</u>

・e で終わる動詞　→　e を取って ing をつける。　例）take → tak<u>ing</u>、use → us<u>ing</u>

・「短母音＋子音」で終わる動詞　→　子音字を重ねて ing をつける。

　　例）stop → sto<u>pping</u>、 drop → dro<u>pping</u>

・ie で終わる動詞　→　ie を y に変えて ing をつける。　例）lie → <u>lying</u>、die → <u>dying</u>

それぞれの進行形が表す主な意味

① 現在進行形は、話し手にとっての現在の時点における〈行動や状態の継続や進行〉を表す。

　　例）He <u>is playing</u> baseball.　彼は（今この時点で）野球をしている。

　　例）I <u>am studying</u> hard this semester.　今学期は一生懸命に勉強している。

※ 現在進行形で〈未来のできごと〉を表すこともある。（p. 66 参照）
※〈状態〉を表す動詞は、進行形にすることができない。

　　例）Tom <u>is knowing</u> Jane. ×　Tom <u>knows</u> Jane. ○

② 過去進行形は、話し手にとっての過去のある時点における〈行動や状態の継続や進行〉を表す。

　　例）She <u>is playing</u> the guitar.　彼女は（いま）ギターを弾いている。

　　　　→　She <u>was playing</u> the guitar then.　彼女はギターを弾いていた。

70　文法解説

③ 未来進行形は、話し手にとっての未来のある時点における〈行動や状態の継続や進行〉を表す。

例）This plane is flying over the Pacific Ocean.

この飛行機は大平洋上空を（いま）飛んでいる。

→ This plane will be flying over the Pacific Ocean at midnight.

この飛行機は真夜中には大平洋上空を飛んでいるだろう。

※ 未来進行形は〈意区や計画を伴わない未来〉も表す。

成り行きや都合で「（自然に）〜することになる」という意味合いを持つ。

例）I'll be seeing you!　そのうちお会いするでしょう。

※ 未来進行形は現在進行中の動作についての推量を表すこともある。

例）It will be raining in Tokyo now.　東京はいま雨が降っているだろう。

④ 現在完了進行形は、過去に始まった動作が現在、あるいはほんの少し前まで継続していることを表す。

例）I have been waiting to see him since ten o'clock.

10 時から（ずっと）彼に会おうと待っています。

⑤ 過去完了進行形は、以前に始まった動作が過去のある時点、あるいはその少し前まで継続していることを表す。

例）He had been sleeping for more than 10 hours when the sun rose.

日が昇ったとき、彼は（それまでに）10 時間以上も寝ていた。

【練習】正しいものを○で囲もう。

1. She (has / is having) lunch now.
2. She (is leaving / leave) next week.
3. At this time tomorrow I (will be / will) having lunch.
4. She (has been / was) studying English for 3 hours.
5. We (had been working / had worked) for 3 hours when our boss called us.

Ⅱ 時の表し方　71

文法解説 Ⅲ

名詞の働きをするもの

名詞とは何か

物、人、事柄などの名前

例）dog　book　love　water

名詞の働き

① 主語・目的語・補語になる

例）These <u>dogs</u> are cute. （主語）これらの犬はかわいい。

I love <u>dogs</u>. （目的語）私は犬が好きだ。

These are cute <u>dogs</u>. （補語）これらはかわいい犬たちだ。

② 前置詞の後ろに置かれて前置詞句となる。

例）Look <u>at that dog</u>. あの犬を見てごらん。

名詞以外で、名詞の働きをするもの

① 準動詞

(1) ~ing（動名詞）

例）<u>Playing</u> video games is fun. テレビゲームをするのは楽しい。

(2) to- 不定詞（名詞用法）

例）<u>To play</u> video games is fun. テレビゲームをするのは楽しい。

② 疑問詞＋ to- 不定詞

例）I don't know <u>where to go</u>. 私はどこへいくべきかわからない。

③ 節

(1) 接続詞 that などに導かれる節

例）I think <u>that he is honest</u>. 私は彼が正直だと思う。

(2) 疑問詞に導かれる節（間接疑問）

例）I don't know <u>when he will come</u>. 彼がいつ来るかわからない。

(3) 関係詞 what / whoever / whatever などに導かれる節

例）I'll do <u>whatever I can do for you</u>.

あなたのためにできることは何でもやります。

III-1　名詞の働きをするもの ①　準動詞

動詞を名詞にするやり方は 2 つある。

① 動詞の原形の前に to をつける（to- 不定詞の名詞用法）

② 動詞の原形に -ing をつける（動名詞）

例）Playing video games is fun. / To play video games is fun.
テレビゲームをするのは楽しい。

※ Play video games. テレビゲームをしなさい。

（is fun をつづけることはできない）

動名詞と to- 不定詞の使い分け

① to- 不定詞は「（今から）〜すること」の意味。よって、〈予定〉や〈願望〉などを表す
動詞の目的語となる。

例）I want to go to the party.　パーティに行きたい。

※ to- 不定詞を目的語にとることができない動詞がいくつかある。代表的なものは
mind（いやがる）、enjoy（楽しむ）、finish（終える）、stop（やめる）など。

② ~ing は「すでに〜したこと」、「今〜していること」の意味。

例）I remember locking the door.
ドアに鍵をかけたことを覚えている。

※ Remember to lock the door.
ドアに鍵をかけるのを覚えておきなさい。　→　忘れずにドアに鍵をかけなさい。

③ 前置詞の後に to- 不定詞をもってくることはできない。

例）I'm fond of to play tennis.　　I'm fond of playing tennis.
×　　　　　　　　　　　　　　○
テニスをするのが好きだ。

【練習】正しいものを○で囲もう。

1. I enjoyed (watching / to watch) the baseball game.

2. I'm planning (going / to go) on a trip next weekend.

3. He is proud of (being / to be) her boyfriend.

Ⅲ 名詞の働きをするもの　73

III–2　名詞の働きをするもの ②　疑問詞＋to- 不定詞

「what, where, when, how などの疑問詞＋to- 不定詞」は、名詞の働きをして、主語・目的語・補語などになる。「〜すべきか（ということ）」と訳すとよい。

例）Tell me <u>what to do</u> next.　次に何をすべきか教えてください。
　　I didn't know <u>when to start</u>.　いつ出発すべきかわからなかった。
　　Do you know <u>how to use</u> this machine?
　　　　　どうやってこの機械を使うべきか（→この機械の使い方）を知っていますか。
　　I didn't know <u>which way to go</u>.　どの道を行くべきかわからなかった。
　　※ この文のように、**疑問詞**が**名詞**を伴うこともある。

主な疑問詞について下の表にまとめておく。

意味	指すもの	主格	所有格	目的格
		（〜は、〜が）	（〜の）	（〜を、〜に）
だれ	人	who	whose	whom (who で代用することもある)
どれ、どちら（の）	人・物	which	—	which
何・どの	物	what	—	what

༺༻༺༻༺༻༺༻༺༻༺༻༺༻༺༻༺༻༺༻༺༻

【練習】正しいものを○で囲もう。

1. I'll show you (why / how) to start up this PC.
2. She asked her teacher (what / when) to do.
3. Please tell me (whose / who) instructions to follow.

III–3　名詞の働きをするもの ③　節（that- 節など）

接続詞 that（〜ということ）、if（〜かどうか）、whether（〜かどうか）に導かれる節も名詞の働きをして、主語・目的語・補語などになる。

例）I know that he is honest.

　　　私は彼が正直だと知っている。

　　※ that- 節は動詞 know の**目的語**「彼が正直だということ」

| that- 節の代わりに置く仮主語 it | that- 節が主語の場合は日常語では**仮主語 it** を用いる。

例）That he won the race is true.　→　**It** is true that he won the race.

　　　彼がそのレースに勝ったというのは本当だ。

| that の省略 |　that- 節の that は省略されることが多い。

例）I think that he is honest.　→　I think he is honest.

　　　私は彼が正直だと思う。

| 時制の一致 |　that- 節の中の述語動詞の時制は**主節の述語動詞**と合わせる。

例）I think that he will come.　私は彼が来ると思う。

　→　I thought that he would come.　私は彼が来ると思った。

| whether と if の使い分け |　「〜かどうか」を意味する if- 節は文頭に置いてはならない。

例）Whether he will pass the exam is not certain. ○

　　If he will pass the exam is not certain. ×

　　　彼が試験に合格するかどうかは確かではない。

※ whether は or ~ や or not を伴うことが多い。

例）I don't know **whether** I should take a bus **or** a taxi.

　　　バスを使うべきかタクシーを使うべきかわからない。

【練習】正しいものを○で囲もう。

1. Do you think (if / that) he will come to the party?

2. She says (if / that) she will become a teacher.

3. It is sad (whether / that) he couldn't pass the exam.

Ⅲ 名詞の働きをするもの　75

III-4　名詞の働きをするもの ④　節（間接疑問）

「what, where, when, how などの疑問詞＋主語＋述語動詞」も名詞の働きをして、主語・目的語・補語などになる。

例）Tell me <u>when he left</u>.　彼が何時に帰ったか教えてください。

間接疑問の語順

間接疑問の中では平叙文と同じく「主語＋述語動詞」となる。

例）When <u>did he leave</u>?　彼は何時に帰りましたか。

（疑問詞 + did (do, does) ＋主語＋動詞の原形）

→　I don't know when he left.

間接疑問中の動詞の時制

that- 節の場合と同じく、間接疑問の中の動詞は**時制の一致**を受ける。

例）I <u>don't know</u> when he <u>left</u>.　彼がいつ帰ったのか知らない。

I <u>didn't know</u> when he <u>had left</u>.　彼がいつ帰ったのか知らなかった。

間接疑問の中の間接疑問

Do you think ~ ? など、yes, no で答えられない疑問文の中で間接疑問が用いられるときには、疑問詞だけが文頭に来る。

例）When <u>do you think</u> he will come?　彼がいつ来ると思いますか。

※ do you think は挿入句とみなされる。

❧❧❧❧❧❧❧❧❧❧❧❧❧❧❧❧❧❧❧❧❧❧❧❧❧❧❧

【練習】正しいものを○で囲もう。

1.　Do you know (when / which) he will come?

2.　I asked him when (he had finished / had he finished) the job.

3.　(What do you know / Do you know what) was given to him?

76　文法解説

III-5　名詞の働きをするもの ⑤　節（関係詞節）

関係詞 what「～する（した）こと」、whatever「～する（した）ものは何でも」(what の強調形)、whoever「～する（した）のはだれでも」などに導かれる節も、名詞の働きをして、主語・目的語・補語などになる。

> 例）Do <u>what he tells you to do</u>.
>
> 　　　彼があなたにやりなさいと言うことをやりなさい。
>
> 　Do <u>whatever he tells you to do</u>.
>
> 　　　彼があなたにやりなさいと言うことは何でもやりなさい。
>
> <u>Whomever [Whoever] you want to invite</u> will be welcome.
>
> ＝ <u>Anyone whom you want to invite</u> will be welcome.
>
> 　　　あなたが招待したい人はだれでも歓迎します。
>
> ※日常英語では whomever は whoever で代用されるのがふつう。

【注意】副詞節を導く whatever, whoever など

whatever / whoever / whomever / whichever に導かれる節は、それぞれ「何が（を）～とも」、「だれが（を）～とも」、「どれ（どちらの…）を～とも」という意味の副詞節になることもある。

> 例）<u>Whatever happens</u>, I won't change my mind.
>
> 　　　何が起ころうと、私の決心は変わらない。

名詞を伴う whichever

whichever は名詞を伴うこともある。

> 例）Take whichever (book) you want.
>
> 　　　欲しい方（の本）を取りなさい。

【練習】正しいものを○で囲もう。

1. (Whoever / Whomever) can swim can apply for the job.
2. Do (whatever / whoever) you want to do.
3. (Whichever / Whoever) way you go, you will regret it.

Ⅲ 名詞の働きをするもの　77

文法解説 Ⅳ

名詞を修飾するもの

名詞を修飾するには次のような方法がある。

① 形容詞

a beautiful **girl**　　きれいな**女の子**

② 前置詞句

a **girl** at the bus stop　　バス停にいる**女の子**

③ 準動詞

(1) 現在分詞

a **girl** singing on the stage　　ステージで歌っている**女の子**

(2) 過去分詞

a **watch** made in Italy　　イタリア製の**時計**）

(3) to- 不定詞（形容詞用法）

a **girl** to help me　　私を手伝ってくれる**女の子**

④ 関係詞

a **girl** who was singing on the stage a while ago

　さきほどステージで歌っていた**女の子**

※ 形容詞は文の補語になる場合もある（文の要素）。

例）I　　bought　a　new　car.　　new は名詞 car を修飾

　主語　述語動詞　　　　目的語　（文の要素ではない）

This　car　　is　　　new.

　主語　述語動詞　補語　（new は文の要素）

78　文法解説

IV-1　名詞を修飾するもの ①　準動詞

動詞が**名詞**を修飾できるようにするには、次の３つの変化のしかたがある。

① 現在分詞
　　例）**a girl** singing on the stage　ステージで歌っている**女の子**
② 過去分詞
　　例）**a watch** made in Italy　イタリア製の**時計**
③ to- 不定詞（形容詞用法）
　　例）**a girl** to help me　私を手伝ってくれる**女の子**

|準動詞の使い分け|

① ~ing（現在分詞）「（今）～している○○（名詞）」
　修飾語句がつく場合は必ず**名詞**の後に置く。
　　例）a singing on the stage girl　×
　　　　a girl singing on the stage　○

② 過去分詞　「～された、～されている○○（名詞）」
　修飾語句がつく場合は必ず**名詞**の後に置く。
　　例）a made in Italy watch　×
　　　　a watch made in Italy　○

③ to- 不定詞（形容詞用法）「（これから）～するための、～すべき○○（名詞）」
　必ず**名詞**の直後に置く。

　※ 不定詞の意味上の**主語**は文の**主語**であることが多い。
　　例）I must find **a place** to sleep.　寝るための場所を見つけなければいけない。
　　　　"to sleep" の意味上の**主語**は "I"

【練習】正しいものを○で囲もう。

1. The picture (taking / taken) in Kyoto is beautiful.
2. Do you have time (to meet / meeting) me?
3. Look at that woman (talking / to talk) with Ken.

IV-2 名詞を修飾するもの ② 関係代名詞

準動詞だけでは**名詞**を修飾する内容を表現しきれない場合は、関係詞を使う。

「**名詞**（先行詞）＋ 関係詞 (who, which, whom, whose, that ~) ＋ (主語) ＋ (述語動詞)」

関係詞は先行詞の種類および**節**の中での役割によって使い分ける。

> 例）I know the **girl** who[that] was singing on the stage a while ago.
>
> 　　 さきほどステージで歌っていた**女の子**を知っています。
>
> This is a **train** which[that] goes to Hakata.　これは博多へ行く**列車**です。
>
> She has a **sister** whose name is Saori.
>
> 　　 彼女にはさおりという名前の**妹**がいます。

関係詞の種類

先行詞の種類	主格	所有格	目的格
人	who that	whose	whom (who) that
物・動物	which that	whose of which	which that
物・動物・人	that		that

※ アメリカ英語では who, whom, which の代わりに that を用いることがある。また、目的格の**関係代名詞**は省略されることが多い。

※ 先行詞に all, every, the only, 最上級の形容詞などが含まれているときには、**関係代名詞** that を用いることが多い。

> 例）This is the only book <u>that</u> I have.　これは私が持っている唯一の本だ。

〜〜〜〜〜〜〜〜〜〜〜〜〜〜〜〜〜〜〜〜〜〜〜〜〜〜〜〜〜〜

【練習】正しいものを○で囲もう。

1. Tom is a college student (which / who) likes playing soccer.
2. I'm reading a letter (whom / which) Akira sent to me.
3. (Which / What) I have lost is my key.

IV–3　名詞を修飾するもの ③　前置詞＋関係代名詞

> 関係代名詞が前置詞を伴うことがある。「名詞（先行詞）＋前置詞＋関係詞～」の語順にする場合と、前置詞を関係代名詞節の最後に置く場合とがある。
>
> 例）I know the girl. Tom was dancing with her.
> 　　→　I know the **girl** (whom [who]) Tom was dancing with.
> 　または　I know the **girl** with whom Tom was dancing.（あらたまった表現）
> 　　　　私はトムが一緒に踊っていた女の子を知っています。

※ 前置詞の直後では that を使うことはできない。また、前置詞の直後の関係代名詞を省略することはできない。
　　例）I know the girl with that Tom was dancing. は不可

【練習】正しいものを○で囲もう。
1. I want to see the house (which / in which) she was born.
2. He is the journalist from (which / whom) I got the information.
3. I like the song (in / to) which you are listening now.

IV–4　名詞を修飾するもの ④　関係副詞

> 〈場所〉や〈時〉を表すときは**関係副詞** (where, when) を用いる。
>
> 例) The **hotel** was very nice. We stayed at the hotel.
>
> 　　at the hotel「そのホテルに」は stayed を修飾する（副詞句）
>
> 　→　The **hotel** where we stayed was very nice.
>
> 　　　私たちが泊まった**ホテル**はとてもすてきだった。
>
> 　　　　→　関係副詞を用いる
>
> 例) I'll never forget the **day**. I first met you on that day.
>
> 　　on that day「その日に」は met you を修飾する（副詞句）
>
> 　→　I'll never forget the **day** when I first met you.
>
> 　　　私はあなたに初めて会った日のことを決して忘れないでしょう。

関係副詞と関係代名詞の使い分け

例) The hotel was very nice. We visited the hotel.　the hotel は visited の**目的語**

　→　The hotel which we visited was very nice.　（目的格の関係代名詞）

　　　私たちが訪れたホテルはとてもすてきだった。

which の代用 that

関係副詞 when の代用として that が用いられることがある。

例) I will never forget the day that [when] my son was born.

　　　息子が生まれた日を私は忘れない。

関係副詞 how, why

例) This is the way (how) it happened.　このようにしてそれは起こりました。〈方法〉

　　Do you know the reason (why) she was absent yesterday?〈理由〉

　　　昨日彼女が休んだ理由をあなたは知っていますか。

※ ふつう the way または how、the reason または why のどちらかが省略される。

【練習】正しいものを〇で囲もう。

1. I want to see the house (which / where) she was born.
2. The year (when / where) we had heavy snow was 1995.
3. This is (how / what) our team won the game.

文法解説 V

名詞以外を修飾するもの

名詞以外のもの、たとえば動詞・形容詞・副詞・句・節を修飾するものは副詞である。副詞のはたらきをする句や節をそれぞれ副詞句・副詞節と言う。

例）I studied hard every day.　私は毎日一生懸命に勉強した。（動詞 studied を修飾）

He was very tired.　彼はとても疲れていた。（形容詞 tired を修飾）

※ 副詞は文の要素（主語・述語動詞・目的語・補語）にはならない。

V–1　名詞以外を修飾するもの ①　副詞・副詞句

to- 不定詞の副詞用法

例）I studied hard to pass the exam.　〈目的〉を表す

私は試験に合格するため一生懸命に勉強した。

He was sad to hear the news.　〈原因・理由〉を表す

彼はその知らせを聞いて悲しんだ。

She grew up to be a scientist.　〈結果〉を表す

彼女は大人になって科学者になった。

He was too surprised to speak.　〈程度〉を表す

私はあまりにも驚いたので声が出なかった。

※ to- 不定詞は意味上の主語（for ＋人）を前に伴うことがある。

例）I gave her a letter for her to read later.

彼女があとで読んでくれるよう、彼女に手紙をわたした。

【練習】正しいものを○で囲もう。

1. I went to the library (to borrow / borrowing) an English book.

2. He was (so / too) tired to do the job.

3. I gave her a sheet of paper (for / to) her to write down my phone number on.

V 名詞以外を修飾するもの　83

V-2　名詞以外を修飾するもの②　分詞構文

> 「~ing（＋修飾語句）」が主節を修飾する役割を果たすことがある。これを**分詞構文**という。
>
> 例）Walking in the park, I met an old friend.　公園を歩いていると、旧友に出会った。

分詞構文が表す主な意味

「～したときに」、「～なので」、「～しながら」、「～すれば」など

例）Feeling very tired, I went to bed early.

とても疲れたので、早めに寝た。

She was cooking dinner, listening to the radio.

彼女はラジオを聞きながら夕食の準備をしていた。

分詞構文の位置

分詞構文は文頭・文中・文末のいずれにも置くことができる

not を伴う分詞構文

not は ~ing の前に置く

例）Not knowing what to do, I called my mother.

どうしていいのかわからなかったので、母に電話した。

having ＋ 過去分詞

「having ＋過去分詞」は主節があらわす時点よりも以前の事柄に言及する際にもちいる。

例）Having finished my homework, I went swimming.

宿題を終わらせたので、泳ぎに行った。

受動態の分詞構文

「being ＋過去分詞」（受動態の分詞構文）の being はふつう省略される。

例）Written in simple English, the book was easy to understand.

簡単な英語で書かれていたので、その本は理解しやすかった。

【練習】正しいものを○で囲もう。

1. I played tennis and (taking / took) a bath.
2. (Arriving / Arrived) at the station, I called him.
3. (Visiting / Having visited) here before, I showed my family around the town.

84　文法解説

V-3　名詞以外を修飾するもの ③　副詞節

副詞節の主なものは次の 2 つである
① 主節を修飾する副詞節（従属節）
　　例）<u>If it is fine tomorrow</u>, I'll go fishing.　明日天気がよければつりに行くつもりだ。
　　　（if- 節は主節 I'll go fishing を修飾）
② 形容詞を修飾する副詞節（接続詞は that）
　　例）He was sure <u>that he would pass the exam.</u>
　　　　彼は試験に合格すると確信していた。（that- 節は形容詞 sure を修飾）

従属節を導く副詞節

① の副詞節を導く接続詞の主なものは、as「〜なので、〜のとき、〜につれて」、because
「〜なので」、if「〜ならば」、though [although]「〜だけれども」
　　例）<u>When</u> he comes, he always stays long.　彼は来るといつも長居する。
　　　　<u>As</u> he was very tired, he went to bed early.　彼はとても疲れていたので早寝した。

so (such) ～ that- 節

「so ＋形容詞または副詞＋ that- 節」または「such ＋（冠詞＋名詞）＋ that- 節」
　　＝「あまりに〜なので…」〈程度〉を表す
　　　例）I was <u>so</u> surprised <u>that I could not speak.</u>
　　　　　私はあまりに驚いたので声が出なかった。

so ～ that- 節

「so that ＋主語 can [may, could, might] ＋動詞の原形」
　　＝「〜が…するように」〈目的〉を表す
　　　例）Her father gave her a lot of money <u>so that she could travel abroad.</u>
　　　　　彼女が海外旅行に行けるように父親は彼女にたくさんのお金を与えた。

【練習】正しいものを○で囲もう。

1. (As / Though) he was very tired, he did his homework.
2. It was (so / such) cold outside that I stayed home all day.
3. He is working very hard (that / so that) he can support his family.

V 名詞以外を修飾するもの　85

文法解説 **VI**

助動詞

動詞に意味を加えたいときには**助動詞**を用い、「**主語＋助動詞＋動詞の原形**」とする。

例）I swim every day.（私は毎日、泳ぎます）→ I **can** swim.（私は泳ぐことが<u>できます</u>）

否定文のつくり方	疑問文のつくり方
助動詞のあとに not をつける。	「助動詞＋主語＋動詞の原形～ ?」の語順
例）I <u>can't (cannot)</u> swim.	例）Can you swim?
私は泳ぐことができません。	泳げますか。

VI-1　助動詞 ①　can, may, will

助動詞	意　味	例
can （過去形は could）	～することができる〈可能〉 ～してもよい〈許可〉	I **can** swim 500 meters. 　　　私は 500 メートル泳ぐことができる。 You **can** use my pen. 　　　私のペンを使っていいですよ。
may （過去形は might）	～してもよい〈許可〉 ～かもしれない〈推量〉	You **may** go home. 　　　帰ってよろしい。 He **may** be sick. 　　　彼は病気かもしれません。
will （過去形は would）	～だろう〈未来〉 ～するつもりだ〈意志〉	It **will** be fine tomorrow. 　　　明日は晴れるでしょう。 I **will** do my best. 　　　最善をつくします。

※ Will you ~ ? / Can you ~ ? / Shall I ~ ? / Shall we ~ ? は〈依頼〉、〈提案〉などの意味を表すことが多い。

例）<u>Will [Can] you</u> open the window?　窓を開けてくれますか。〈依頼〉

<u>Shall I</u> open the window?　窓を開けましょうか。〈提案〉

<u>Shall we</u> dance?　踊りましょうか。〈提案〉

【練習】正しいものを○で囲もう。

1. We (can / may) see the ocean from here.　ここから海が見えます。

2. You (may / shall) smoke here.　ここでタバコを吸ってもいいですよ。

3. (May / Will) you be quiet, please?　静かにしてくれませんか。

86　文法解説

VI–2　助動詞 ②　must, should, need

must, should, need などの助動詞を用いて、〈義務〉や〈必要〉の意味を表すことができる。

助動詞	意　味	例
must	〜しなければならない 〈義務〉	You **must** take that train. 　　あの列車に乗らないといけません。〈義務〉
	〜にちがいない 〈確信〉	He **must** be home. 　　彼は家にいるにちがいありません。〈確信〉
	（否定文で）〜してはいけない〈禁止〉	You **must not [mustn't]** go home. 　　家に帰ってはいけません。〈禁止〉 ※「家に帰る必要はない」と言いたい時は **don't have to 〜** や **don't need to 〜** を使う。
should	〜すべきである 〈義務〉	You **should** watch your weight. 　　あなたは体重に気をつけるべきです。
need	〜する必要がある　〈必要〉 ※疑問文と否定文で使用	**Need** I tell him? No, you **need not [needn't]**. 　　彼に言う必要はありますか。いや、ありません。

※ be able to 〜「〜することができる」, have to 〜「〜しなければならない」, ought to 〜「〜すべきである」 など、助動詞と類似の意味を表すことのできる表現がある。
　　例）The baby will be able to walk soon.
　　　　　その赤ちゃんはすぐに歩けるようになるだろう。
　　　　I had to take that train.　あの列車に乗らなければいけなかった。
　　　　You ought to give your seat to elderly people.　お年寄りに席をゆずるべきだ。

※「should have ＋過去分詞」、「must have ＋過去分詞」はそれぞれ「〜すべきだった（がしなかった）」、「〜したにちがいない」という意味になる。
　　例）I should have taken that train.
　　　　　あの列車に乗るべきだった。（実際には乗らなかった）

【練習】正しいものを○で囲もう。

1.　(Have / Must) I apologize to him?（apologize ＝ あやまる）

2.　You (have / should) come at once.

3.　We will (ought / have) to get up early tomorrow.

文法解説 Ⅶ

受 動 態

「be 動詞＋過去分詞」で、「～される、～されている」の意味を表す。

能動態の文を受動態の文に変えるやり方は次の通り。

Everybody loves John.　　誰もがジョンを好きだ。

動詞　→　be 動詞＋過去分詞

John is loved **by everybody**.　ジョンは誰からも好かれている。

受動態に用いる前置詞

受動態につづく前置詞は by とは限らない。

例）He is known to all the students in this school.

彼はこの学校のすべての学生に知られている。

The ground was covered with snow.　　地面は雪でおおわれていた。

by ～ の省略

by them, by you, by us などはふつう省略される。

例）What language is spoken in Brazil?　　ブラジルでは何語が話されていますか。

補語がある文の受動態

補語などがある場合には、受動態のあとにつづける。

例）We call him Kenny.　　私たちは彼をケニーと呼んでいる。

　→　He is called Kenny.　　彼はケニーと呼ばれている。

【練習】正しいものを○で囲もう。

1.　The report should (finish / be finished) by Monday.

2.　Tom (lives / is lived) with his mother.

3.　We (named / were named) the dog John.

88　文法解説

文法解説 Ⅷ

比 較

２つ以上のものや２人以上の人を比較するときには、**形容詞や副詞の形を変えればよい。**

Ⅷ-1　比較 ①　原級比較

「～と同じくらい…」という、原級比較の文を作るには、**形容詞や副詞の前後に** as **をおけ**ばよい。

例）Jane is <u>as</u> clever <u>as</u> Tom.

　　　ジェーンはトムと同じくらい利口だ。

　　Jane is studying <u>as</u> hard <u>as</u> Tom.

　　　ジェーンはトムと同じくらい一生懸命に勉強している。

---

not so [as] ~ as

not がある場合には、「～ほど…ない」の意味になる。

例）Jane is <u>not as [so]</u> clever <u>as</u> Tom.

　　　ジェーンはトムほど利口ではない。

　　（not as ~ as の代わりに not so ~ as が用いられることもある）

倍数を表す as ~ as ...

倍数を表す場合には、as の前に序数 (twice, three times, four times …) を置けばよい。

例）The population of Tokyo is <u>twice as</u> big <u>as</u> that of my hometown.

　　　東京の人口は私のふるさとの町の２倍だ。

【練習】正しいものを○で囲もう。

1. He can (swim as fast / as fast swim) as Greg.
2. He has (many as / as many) books as Greg.
3. He has (as many three times / three times as many) books as Greg.

Ⅷ 比較　89

VIII–2　比較 ②　比較級、最上級

> 「～よりも…」、「もっとも…」という、比較級や最上級を用いた文を作るには、**形容詞や副詞**にそれぞれ -er、-est をつければよい。
>
> 　例）Jane is <u>cleverer</u> than Tom.
> 　　　　　　ジェーンはトムより利口だ。
> 　　　Jane is <u>the cleverest</u> of all her classmates.
> 　　　　　　ジェーンは同級生たちの中でもっとも利口だ。

比較級と最上級のつくりかた

(1) 1 音節の語の大部分および 2 音節語の一部　原級の語尾に -er、-est をつける

　　例）small → small<u>er</u> → small<u>est</u>

　※ hot → hot<u>ter</u> → hot<u>test</u>、 pretty → pret<u>tier</u> → pret<u>tiest</u> などのように、語尾の字を重ねたり、y を i に変える場合もある。

(2) 2 音節の語の一部および 3 音節以上の語　more / most をつける

　　例）exciting → more exciting → most exciting

※ 2 音節の単語の場合は、(1) と (2) のどちらのパターンであるかを辞書で確認しよう。
※ 不規則活用をする語は次の通り。

　　good, well → better → best　　　　bad, ill → worse → worst
　　little → less → least　　　　many, much → more → most

---

the のない最上級の形容詞

最上級の形容詞には the をつけるのがふつうだが、同一人・同一物の中で比較を行っている場合には the をつけない。

　　例）She is happiest when she is knitting.　彼女は編物をしているときが一番幸せだ。

【練習】正しいものを○で囲もう。

1. He is (as tall / taller / tallest) than Tom.
2. She speaks English (well / better / best) than anyone else in her class.
3. This book is (interesting / more interesting) than that one.

90　文法解説

文法解説 Ⅸ

仮定法

「もし〜なら、…だろう」、「もし〜だったら、…だっただろう」という〈仮定〉の表現には仮定法を用いる。

Ⅸ–1　仮定法 ①　仮定法過去・仮定法過去完了

① 仮定法過去（現在の事実に反することや、現在・未来において実現しがたいことについて述べる）

「If + 主語 + 述語動詞（過去形）…，主語 + 助動詞の過去形 + 動詞の原形 …」

例）If I were rich, I would travel around the world.

もし金持ちなら世界中を旅行するのだが。

※ be 動詞は主語にかかわりなく were が使われることが多い。

② 仮定法過去完了（過去の事実に反することについて述べる）

「If + 主語 + 述語動詞（過去完了），主語 + 助動詞の過去形 + have + 過去分詞」

例）If I had been rich, I would have traveled around the world.

もし金持ちだったら世界中を旅行したのだが。

仮定法で用いられる助動詞の意味

・would（will の過去形）「〜だろう」

・could（can の過去形）「〜できる」、「〜することがあり得る」

・might（may の過去形）「〜かもしれない」

・should（shall の過去形）（I, we を主語にして）「〜だろう」

（「〜すべき、きっと〜だ」を意味する助動詞 should と混同しないよう気をつけよう）

※「If があるから仮定法、ないから直説法」とはかぎらない。

例）If it is fine tomorrow, I will go fishing.《直説法》

明日晴れれば、釣りに行くつもりだ。（晴れる可能性が十分にある）

【練習】正しいものを○で囲もう。

1. If I (am / were) rich, I would buy a house.

2. If I (had / were) been 10 years younger, I would have proposed to her.

3. If it rains, we (will / would) cancel the hiking.

Ⅸ 仮定法　91

IX-2　仮定法 ②　I wish ~

> 「～ならよいのになあ」、「～だったらよかったのになあ」という〈願望〉を表すには、I wish … を用いる。普通はその後に that- 節（that は省略される）が続くが、その場合、動詞は**過去形**または**過去完了形**にする。

I wish ~ 構文の主な意味

① **仮定法過去**〈現在の事実に反する願望〉

　例）<u>I wish</u> I were a bird.　鳥だったらいいのにな。

　　　<u>I wish</u> I could swim.　泳げたらいいのにな。

② **仮定法過去完了**〈過去の事実に反する願望〉

　例）<u>I wish</u> I had studied more in my high school days.

　　　　高校時代にもっと勉強しておけばよかったのにな。

　　<u>I wish</u> I could have gone on a trip with you last summer.

　　　　去年の夏あなたと一緒に旅行できたらよかったのにな。

※ wish があっても**仮定法**とは限らないので注意すること。

　例）<u>I wish</u> you a merry Christmas.　楽しいクリスマスでありますように。

　　　<u>I wish</u> to see the professor.　その教授にお会いしたい。

〜〜〜〜〜〜〜〜〜〜〜〜〜〜〜〜〜〜〜〜〜〜〜〜〜〜〜〜〜〜〜

【練習】正しいものを〇で囲もう。

1. I'm sorry you are busy now. I wish you (could / can) come with me.

2. I made 3 mistakes in the math test. I wish I (got / had got) full marks.

3. I wish you (had invited / invited) me to the party. Everybody says it was great.

巻末付録 2

不規則動詞の活用
一覧表

★不規則動詞の活用　一覧表

原形（意味）	過去形	過去分詞形
be [am, are, is]（〜である）	was / were	been
become（〜になる）	became	become
begin（始める）	began	begun
bring（持ってくる）	brought	brought
buy（買う）	bought	bought
catch（つかまえる）	caught	caught
come（来る）	came	come
cut（切る）	cut	cut
do [does]（する）	did	done
draw（描く、引く）	drew	drawn
drink（飲む）	drank	drunk
drive（運転する）	drove	driven
eat（食べる）	ate	eaten
fall（落ちる、倒れる）	fell	fallen
feel（感じる）	felt	felt
fight（戦う）	fought	fought
find（見つける）	found	found
fly（飛ぶ）	flew	flown
forget（忘れる）	forgot	forgotten (forgot)
get（得る、〜になる、移動する）	got	got (gotten)
give（与える）	gave	given
go（行く）	went	gone
grow（育つ、育てる、〜になる）	grew	grown
have [has]（持っている）	had	had
hear（聞こえる）	heard	heard
hit（打つ）	hit	hit
hold（手に持つ、開催する）	held	held
hurt（傷つける、痛む）	hurt	hurt
keep（保つ、〜し続ける）	kept	kept
know（知っている）	knew	known
leave（去る、残す）	left	left

lend（貸す）	lent	lent
lie（横になる）	lay	lain
lose（失う）	lost	lost
make（作る、～になる、～させる）	made	made
meet（会う）	met	met
oversleep（寝坊する）	overslept	overslept
pay（支払う）	paid	paid
put（置く）	put	put
read（読む）	read（発音に注意）	read（発音に注意）
ride（乗る）	rode	ridden
rise（上がる、昇る）	rose	risen
run（走る）	ran	run
say（言う）	said	said
see（見える、会う）	saw	seen
sell（売る）	sold	sold
send（送る）	sent	sent
set（据える）	set	set
shoot（撃つ、急上昇する）	shot	shot
show（見せる）	showed	shown (showed)
sing（歌う）	sang	sung
sit（座る）	sat	sat
sleep（眠る）	slept	slept
speak（話す）	spoke	spoken
spend（(金・時間を)使う）	spent	spent
spread（広げる、広がる）	spread	spread
stand（立っている）	stood	stood
swim（泳ぐ）	swam	swum
take（取る、選ぶ、必要とする）	took	taken
teach（教える）	taught	taught
tell（言う、話す）	told	told
think（思う、考える）	thought	thought
throw（投げる）	threw	thrown
understand（理解する）	understood	understood
wear（身に着けている）	wore	worn
write（書く）	wrote	written

What Really Happened?
—World Mysteries Solved—

ほんと？うそ？ 世界のびっくりミステリー

[検印廃止]

2016 年 2 月 1 日　初版発行　　2022 年 3 月 10 日　第 5 刷発行

著　　者　　Ｆｒａｎｋ　　Ｂａｉｌｅｙ
　　　　　　納　冨　未　世
　　　　　　田　宮　晴　彦
　　　　　　高　本　孝　子
発　行　者　　丸　小　雅　臣
組　　版　　ほ　ん　の　し　ろ
印刷・製本　　創　栄　図　書　印　刷

〒162–0065　東京都新宿区住吉町 8–9
発行所　開文社出版株式会社
TEL 03–3358–6288　　FAX 03–3358–6287
www.kaibunsha.co.jp

ISBN978–4–87571–729–4 C1382